Gr   ov

Stage 15

Teaching Notes

Lindsay Pickton and Christine Chen

OXFORD
UNIVERSITY PRESS

Contents

A United Force

Beware of the Vikings

Gladiator

Lion of Africa

Master Leonardo

Riches of the Amazon

Introduction

TreeTops *Graphic Novels* are action-packed adventure stories especially selected to motivate and engage 7–11 year old readers. They combine historical periods and real people with fictional characters to enhance accessibility. Additionally, these vivid narratives contain non-fiction pages that provide context to inform and emphasise each story's factual basis.

The content of these Graphic Novels has been levelled to the TreeTops Stages. TreeTops Stages follow on from the Oxford Reading Tree Stages and are designed to be used flexibly to match to individual pupils' reading ability.

Using graphic novels in the classroom

Graphic Novels can support less able readers due to their reduced word-count and the fact that the pictures scaffold much of the meaning. The exciting comic-book style motivates many reluctant readers and may well attract children who have previously not enjoyed fiction. However, these books are not intended for any particular pupil group, they can be both suitable and exciting for anyone and may make popular additions to the class library.

In using the books for group or individual teaching, all the usual book-reading comprehension strategies can be used, such as making predictions from the cover and blurb, and briefly walking through the text to get a sense of the story. Additionally, graphic stories have unique features that can be used to explore the story more fully, such as use of facial expression, body language, the way the artist has chosen to lay out a scene, the choice of speech or thought bubble, sound effects and so on. The ways in which pictures describe characters, create atmosphere and help to structure plot should be discussed, as these are stories told graphically rather than novels with illustrations. Children should be encouraged to provide evidence for their opinions with a combination of words and pictures. The factual 'Time Out' pages can be used to further enhance and develop comprehension of the story and its themes.

The graphic focus on facial expression and body language creates a direct link with role play, and it is recommended that these stories provide stimulus for drama. The recreation of scenes via 'freeze-framing' will help develop children's understanding of character and motivation; if these scenes are photographed and children are shown how to add their own speech and thought bubbles on screen, they will be developing ICT skills while improving literal and inferential comprehension. Moreover, this highly motivating process can have direct impact on the quality of boys' writing.

Using this Teaching Notes booklet

This booklet provides suggestions for using the graphic novels to develop comprehension with children individually or in groups. Suggestions are provided for a range of follow-on activities and cross-curricular links: the factual basis of the stories makes for obvious links with Geography and History.

In order to support planning and record keeping, the curriculum coverage chart on pages 7–9 provides curriculum information relating to the curricula for England, Wales, Northern Ireland and Scotland. This includes PNS Literacy Framework objectives and Assessment Focuses for reading, writing, speaking and listening showing what levels children can reasonably be expected to be achieving when reading these TreeTops books.

Comprehension strategies

Book Title	Comprehension strategy taught through these Teaching Notes					
	Predicting	Questioning	Clarifying	Summarising	Imagining	Deducing
A United Force	✓		✓	✓	✓	✓
Beware of the Vikings	✓		✓	✓	✓	✓
Gladiator	✓	✓	✓	✓	✓	✓
Lion of Africa	✓	✓	✓	✓	✓	✓
Master Leonardo	✓		✓	✓	✓	✓
Riches of the Amazon	✓		✓	✓	✓	✓

Curriculum coverage chart

Legend:
- C = Language comprehension
- V = Vocabulary enrichment
- AF = Assessment Focus
- Y = Year   P = Primary

A United Force	Speaking, listening, drama	Reading	Writing
PNS Literacy Framework (Y6)	(Y6) 1.1, 4.1	V C (Y6) 7.2	(Y6) 9.3, 9.5
National Curriculum	Level 4/5 AF1, 5	Level 4/5 AF1, 2, 3, 6	Level 4/5 AF2, 3, 6, 7
Scotland (P7) (5–14) C for E	Level D Second level	Level D Second level	Level D Second level
N. Ireland (P7/Y7)	1, 3, 4, 5, 7, 8, 9	1, 3, 6, 9, 10, 12, 13	1, 2, 4, 6, 9, 10, 12
Wales (Y6)	Range: 4, 5, 6, 7, 8 Skills: 1, 2, 3, 4, 5, 6	Range: 1, 2, 3, 4 Skills: 1, 2, 3, 4, 5, 6b, 8	Range: 1, 2, 3 Skills: 1, 2, 4, 5, 9
Beware of the Vikings			
PNS Literacy Framework (Y6)	(Y6) 3.2, 4.1	V C (Y6) 7.2	(Y6) 9.3, 9.5
National Curriculum	Level 4/5 AF4, 5	Level 4/5 AF1, 2, 3, 6	Level 4/5 AF2, 3, 6, 7
Scotland (P7) (5–14) C for E	Level D Second level	Level D Second level	Level D Second level
N. Ireland (P7/Y7)	1, 3, 4, 5, 7, 8, 9	1, 3, 6, 9, 10, 12, 13	1, 2, 4, 6, 9, 10, 12
Wales (Y6)	Range: 4, 5, 6, 7, 8 Skills: 1, 2, 3, 4, 5, 6	Range: 1, 2, 3, 4 Skills: 1, 2, 3, 4, 5, 6b, 8	Range: 1, 2, 3 Skills: 1, 2, 4, 5, 9

Curriculum coverage chart

Legend:
- **C** = Language comprehension
- **V** = Vocabulary enrichment
- AF = Assessment Focus
- Y = Year   P = Primary

Gladiator	Speaking, listening, drama	Reading	Writing
PNS Literacy Framework (Y6)	(Y6) 3.2, 4.1	**V C** (Y6) 7.2	**V C** (Y6) 9.3, 9.5
National Curriculum	Level 4/5 AF4, 5	Level 4/5 AF1, 2, 3, 6	Level 4/5 AF2, 3, 7
Scotland (P7) (5–14) C for E	Level D Second level	Level D Second level	Level D Second level
N. Ireland (P7/Y7)	1, 3, 4, 5, 7, 8	1, 3, 6, 9, 10, 12, 13	1, 2, 4, 6, 10, 12
Wales (Y6)	Range: 4, 5, 6, 7, 8 Skills: 1, 2, 3, 4, 5, 6	Range: 1, 2, 3, 4 Skills: 1, 2, 3, 4, 5, 6b, 8	Range: 1, 2, 3 Skills: 1, 2, 4, 5, 9
Lion of Africa			
PNS Literacy Framework (Y6)	(Y6) 1.1, 4.1	**V C** (Y6) 7.2	**V C** (Y6) 9.3, 9.4
National Curriculum	Level 4/5 AF3, 5	Level 4/5 AF1, 2, 3, 6	Level 4/5 AF1, 2, 3
Scotland (P7) (5–14) C for E	Level D Second level	Level D Second level	Level D Second level
N. Ireland (P7/Y7)	1, 3, 4, 5, 7, 8, 9	1, 3, 6, 9, 10, 12, 13	1, 2, 4, 6, 9, 10, 12
Wales (Y6)	Range: 4, 5, 6, 7, 8 Skills: 1, 2, 3, 4, 5, 6	Range: 1, 2, 3, 4 Skills: 1, 2, 3, 4, 5, 6b, 8	Range: 1, 2, 3 Skills: 1, 2, 4, 5, 9

Curriculum coverage chart

Legend:
- **C** = Language comprehension
- **V** = Vocabulary enrichment
- AF = Assessment Focus
- Y = Year P = Primary

	Speaking, listening, drama	Reading	Writing
Master Leonardo			
PNS Literacy Framework (Y6)	(Y6) 4.1	**V C** (Y6) 7.2	(Y6) 9.4, 9.5
National Curriculum	Level 4/5 AF5	Level 4/5 AF1, 2, 3, 6	Level 4/5 AF2, 3, 6, 7
Scotland (P7) (5–14) C for E	Level D Second level	Level D Second level	Level D Second level
N. Ireland (P7/Y7)	1, 3, 4, 5, 7, 8, 9	1, 3, 6, 9, 10, 12, 13	1, 2, 4, 6, 9, 10, 12
Wales (Y6)	Range: 4, 5, 6, 7, 8 Skills: 1, 2, 3, 4, 5, 6	Range: 1, 2, 3, 4 Skills: 1, 2, 3, 4, 5, 6b, 8	Range: 1, 2, 3 Skills: 1, 2, 4, 5, 9
Riches of the Amazon			
PNS Literacy Framework (Y6)	(Y6) 1.1, 4.1	**V C** (Y6) 7.2	(Y6) 9.4, 9.5
National Curriculum	Level 4/5 AF3, 5	Level 4/5 AF1, 2, 3,6	Level 4/5 AF2, 3, 6, 7
Scotland (P7) (5–14) C for E	Level D Second level	Level D Second level	Level D Second level
N. Ireland (P7/Y7)	1,2, 3, 4, 5, 7, 8, 9, 10	1, 3, 6, 9, 10, 12, 13	1, 2, 4, 6, 10, 12
Wales (Y6)	Range: 4, 5, 6, 7, 8 Skills: 1, 2, 3, 4, 5, 6	Range: 1, 2, 3, 4 Skills: 1, 2, 3, 4, 5, 6b, 8	Range: 1, 2, 3 Skills: 1, 2, 4, 5, 9

Cross-curricular links

TreeTops Graphic Novels Stage 15	Cross-curricular link
A United Force	**Art & Design 1c** collect visual … information … to develop their ideas…
Beware the Vikings	**ICT 3a** to share … information in a variety of forms …
Gladiator	**D&T 1b** develop ideas … what they want their design to achieve
Lion of Africa	**History 2b** about social … ethnic diversity of societies studied …
Master Leonardo	**History 1a** place events, people … into correct periods of time
Riches of the Amazon	**Music 2b** explore … organise musical ideas …

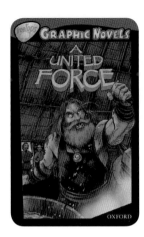

A United Force

Author: Liam O'Donnell

Illustrator: Mike Rooth

Synopsis

This is the story of the first, short-lived Roman invasion of Britain, by Julius Caesar, as seen through the eyes of two Celt boys, Ross and Niall. The boys are constantly getting into trouble, but their desire for adventure leads them towards some very important information about the invaders, and they eventually prove invaluable in the repelling of the invaders.

R, AF = Reading Assessment Focus   **C** = Language comprehension

W, AF = Writing Assessment Focus   **V** = Vocabulary enrichment

S&L, AF = Speaking and Listening Assessment Focus

Group or guided reading

Introducing the book

C *(Imagining)* Look at the front cover together. Ask the children what things Celtic warriors do to make themselves seem fierce.

C *(Predicting)* Ask the children to consider the title: who are they uniting against?

C *(Predicting)* Read the blurb together and predict the ambitions of a general.

C Skim through Chapter 1 to ensure familiarity with the format.

C Look at the characters on page 2. Note real and fictional people.

C *(Imagining)* Stress the importance of 'reading' the pictures as well as the words, e.g. top of page 11, ask: *What might the boys be thinking?*

C Note the Time Out sections and explain their function as fact pages, informing the reader of the realities and context behind the story.

Strategy Check

V Remind the children to use sounds, familiar words-within-words, sentence and story context *and* the illustrations to make sense of unfamiliar words or phrases.

V Note the glossary on page 48 and model how to use it.

During reading

C *(Deducing)* Ask the children to read Chapter 1, including the Time Out on page 13, and to focus on the boys' relationship.

● *(R, AF1)* As the children read independently, listen to each of them in turn, noting and prompting decoding strategies.

Independent Reading

Objective Understand underlying themes, causes and points of view (7.2).

Deducing, Clarifying

- Once the children have read Chapter 1, ask them to pair up and discuss briefly what we know about the boys' friendship.
- Ask the children what the difference in the boys' clothing tells us.
- As a group, discuss the importance of Niall's nobility in this chapter. Does it have an effect on the friendship?
- How does Ross differ from Niall in terms of behaviour?
- On page 12, how has the artist made Niall's father seem particularly fierce?

Assessment Check that the children:

- *(R, AF2&3)* can identify that Niall's status gives him advantages.
- *(R, AF3)* can see that Ross is a greater risk-taker than his friend.

Returning and responding to the text

Objective Understand underlying themes, causes and points of view (7.2).

Summarising, Clarifying, Deducing

- When the children have read the whole story, ask them to summarise how the boys' helped repel the Romans.
- Ask the children to explain the change in Niall's manner from page 15 to page 17.
- Look at pages 20–21. Why was the Roman fighting style so successful?

- Look at pages 24–28. What is the importance of the boys' tour of the village?
- Ask the children to explain the urgency of the boys' message on page 39.
- What might have happened if the weather had been better?
- Ask the children to evaluate the effectiveness of the Time Out information pages. Which of these was the most useful?

Assessment Check that the children:

- (R, AF2) can summarise the boys' contributions to the struggle throughout the story.
- (R, AF3) understand that the Romans were defeated in part by the elements.
- (R, AF6) can comment on the book's purpose of informing readers about Celtic life, and the first Roman invasion.

Speaking and listening activities

Objective Improvise using a range of drama strategies to explore themes (4.1).

- Ask pairs of children to take the roles of the two legionaries at the top of page 32 and continue their discussion about the pros and cons of the invasion.

Assessment (S&L, AF5) Can the children sustain roles to explore ideas and issues?

Objective Use a range of oral techniques to present persuasive arguments (1.1).

- Ask a pair of children to take the roles of Niall and Ross and have them recount the detail of their adventure, as if to the Celtic council.

Assessment *(S&L, AF1)* Can the children talk purposefully and imaginatively to explore ideas and feelings?

Writing activities

Objective Establish, balance and maintain viewpoints (9.3).

- Ask the children to create a 'Celtic newspaper', reporting the repulsion of the Romans. Include speech by main characters.

Assessment *(W, AF2&3)* Can the children write in a formal journalistic style with a specific audience in mind?

Objective Integrate words, images and sounds imaginatively (9.5).

- Ask the children to choose one action-based scene from the story and describe it using precise verbs and adverbial phrases to capture the action.

Assessment *(W, AF6&7)* Can the children apply appropriate word choices alongside grammatical skill to convey a scene in writing?

Cross-curricular links

History

- Research the successful Roman invasion of Britain of 43AD for an additional Time Out page.

Art/Design

- Research Celtic designs and create original versions.

Drama/ICT

- Recreate key scenes via dramatic freeze-framing. Take photos of the freeze-frames and have children add speech and thought bubbles using paper or on screen, creating photo-story versions of the graphic novel.

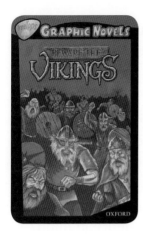

Beware of the Vikings

Author: David Boyd

Illustrator: Mike Rooth

Synopsis

This book imagines the story behind the historical Norse discovery of North America. A fierce Viking, banished for a crime he didn't commit, his loyal friends and young stowaway son search for new land to make home. Their journey takes them through dangerously icy seas to new land and initially friendly Native Americans, who eventually turn on the newcomers.

R, AF = Reading Assessment Focus

W, AF = Writing Assessment Focus

S&L, AF = Speaking and Listening Assessment Focus

C = Language comprehension

V = Vocabulary enrichment

Group or guided reading

Introducing the book

C *(Imagining)* Look at the front cover together and ask the children how the artist has made the Vikings look fierce.

C *(Predicting)* Read the blurb together and ask the children to predict problems on Thorfinn's voyage.

C Skim through Chapter 1 to ensure the children are familiar with the format.

C Look at the characters on page 2. Note real and fictional people.

C *(Imagining)* Stress the importance of 'reading' the pictures as well as the words, e.g. middle of page 10, ask: *How is Thorfinn's popularity shown in the picture?*

C Note the Time Out sections and explain their function as fact pages, informing the reader of the realities and context behind the story.

Strategy Check

V Remind the children to use sounds, familiar words-within-words, sentence and story context *and* the illustrations to make sense of unfamiliar words or phrases.

V Note the glossary on page 48 and model how to use it.

During reading

C *(Deducing)* Ask the children to read Chapter 1, including the Time Out on page 13, and to form an opinion about Thorfinn's character.

● *(R, AF1)* As the children read independently, listen to each of them in turn, noting and prompting decoding strategies.

Independent Reading

Objective   Understand underlying themes, causes and points of view (7.2).

Deducing, Clarifying

- Once the children have read Chapter 1, ask them to pair up and discuss briefly Thorfinn's guilt or innocence.
- Discuss opinions on the fairness of the trial (see 'Viking Laws' Time Out). Was this a fair way of finding guilt?
- How is Thorfinn's popularity made clear?
- On page 12, why does one of the Vikings say 'Like father, like son'?

Assessment   Check that the children:

- (R, AF2) can use the information to assess Thorfinn's guilt.
- (R, AF3) can infer Thorfinn's popularity from the behaviour of the other men.

Returning and responding to the text

Objective   Understand underlying themes, causes and points of view (7.2).

Summarising, Imagining, Deducing

- When the children have read the whole story, ask them to summarise what they have learnt about Vikings.
- Look together at pages 18 and 26. Ask the children to discuss what they learnt from the occasions when the Vikings work together to overcome a problem.
- What is happening in the picture sequence at the bottom of page 25?

- Ask the children to explain how the Vikings make friends with the Native Americans and why that friendship turns sour.
- Why is Thorfinn asked to return home and why does the decision take him over an hour?
- Ask the children to evaluate the effectiveness of the Time Out information pages. Which of these was the most useful?

Assessment Check that the children:

- *(R, AF2)* can summarise learning about the Vikings.
- *(R, AF3)* can infer Thorfinn's reluctance to go back.
- *(R, AF6)* can comment on the book's purpose of informing readers about Vikings, and their discovery of North America.

Speaking and listening activities

Objective Improvise using a range of drama strategies to explore themes (4.1).

- Ask pairs of children to take the roles of Snorri and Thorfinn and improvise a reunion after Snorri is discovered on board the ship.

Assessment *(S&L, AF5)* Can the children sustain roles to explore ideas and issues?

Objective Use a variety of ways to criticise constructively and respond to criticism (3.2).

- Organise groups to take roles as the Viking band and debate whether they should go back home (see page 43).

Assessment *(S&L, AF4)* Can the children make a range of contributions to a group and draw ideas together?

Writing activities

Objective Establish, balance and maintain viewpoints (9.3).

- Guide the children to write a 1960 newspaper report, revealing the exciting new evidence that Vikings landed in America nearly 500 years before Columbus.

Assessment *(W, AF2&3)* Can the children write in a formal journalistic style with a specific audience in mind?

Objective Integrate words, images and sounds imaginatively (9.5).

- Ask the children to describe one action-based scene from the story using precise verbs and adverbial phrases.

Assessment *(W, AF6&7)* Can the children apply appropriate word choices alongside grammatical skill to convey a scene?

Cross-curricular links

Geography
- Work out the route the Viking band took using a globe and world map. Label the map with sites of possible story incidents.

History
- Research the Norse settlement in America for an additional Time Out page.

Drama/ICT
- Recreate key scenes via dramatic freeze-framing. Take photos of the freeze-frames and have children add speech and thought bubbles using paper or on screen, creating photo-story versions of the graphic novel.

Gladiator

Author: Glen Downey

Illustrator: Andrew Barr

Synopsis

Marcus is a young Roman who dreams of avenging the murder of his father by a gladiator. When captured as a slave and sold as a trainee gladiator, he trains hard and becomes successful, fighting to regain his freedom, to rescue his enslaved mother, and eventually to avenge his father.

R, AF = Reading Assessment Focus

W, AF = Writing Assessment Focus

S&L, AF = Speaking and Listening Assessment Focus

C = Language comprehension

V = Vocabulary enrichment

Group or guided reading

Introducing the book

(C) *(Predicting)* Look at the front cover together and ask the children to predict the subject matter of the story.

(C) *(Predicting)* Read the blurb together and predict how Marcus might be separated from his mother and what happened to his father.

(C) *(Clarifying)* Read the introduction on pages 4 and 5 together and ensure the children understand that gladiators were slaves, then skim through Chapter 1 to check familiarity with the format.

(C) Look at the characters on page 2. Note real and fictional people.

(C) *(Imagining)* Stress the importance of 'reading' the pictures as well as the words, e.g. top of page 9, ask: *How does the image show us Marcus is upset?*

(C) Note the Time Out sections and explain their function as fact pages, informing the reader of the realities and context behind the story.

Strategy Check

(V) Remind the children to use sounds, familiar words-within-words, sentence and story context *and* the illustrations to make sense of unfamiliar words or phrases.

(V) Note the glossary on page 48 and model how to use it.

During reading

(C) *(Deducing)* Ask the children to read Chapter 1, including the Time Out on page 13, and to think about what we learn about Marcus.

- *(R, AF1)* As the children read independently, listen to each of them in turn, one-to-one, noting and prompting decoding strategies.

Independent Reading

Objective Understand underlying themes, causes and points of view (7.2).

Deducing, Imagining

- Once the children have read Chapter 1, ask them to pair up and list what is known about Marcus.
- On page 11, discuss reasons for Marcus' sudden aggression.
- On page 9, why is there a ghostly centurion next to Marcus at the bottom of the page?
- Why did the soldiers come for Marcus' father and now his mother?
- Comment on the choice of colours used to illustrate Marcus' flashbacks on pages 7 and 8?

Assessment Check that the children:

- *(R, AF2)* can see the link between the reasons for the parents' arrest.
- *(R, AF3)* understand that Marcus' unhappy memories lead to aggression.

Returning and responding to the text

Objective Understand underlying themes, causes and points of view (7.2).

Summarising, Deducing, Clarifying

- When the children have read the whole story, ask their opinions on what motivated Marcus to become a successful gladiator.
- Ask the children to explain why Marcus was selected for gladiator school.

- On page 33, why is Marcus impatient to fight again?
- What opinions do the children have about the bloodthirstiness of the Roman spectators?
- Discuss the impact of the use of red in fight scenes.
- Ask the children to evaluate the effectiveness of the Time Out information pages. Which of these was the most useful?

Assessment Check that the children:

- *(R, AF3)* can explain Marcus' success with reference to his past and goals.
- *(R, AF2)* understand the popularity of Roman gladiators, with reference to modern sports.
- *(R, AF6)* can comment on the book's purpose of informing readers about the position of slaves and gladiators in Roman society.

Speaking and listening activities

Objective Improvise using a range of drama strategies to explore themes (4.1).

- Ask pairs of children to take the roles of Marcus and his mother following his final victory, improvising their reunion.

Assessment *(S&L, AF5)* Can the children sustain roles to explore ideas and issues?

Objective Use a variety of ways to criticise constructively and respond to criticism (3.2).

- Organise a debate about the rights and wrongs of violent spectator sports, ancient and modern.

Assessment *(S&L, AF4)* Can the children make a range of contributions to a group and draw ideas together?

Writing activities

Objective Establish, balance and maintain viewpoints (9.3).

- Ask the children to write a balanced argument for and against a violent spectator sport (ancient or modern, with a decisive conclusion).

Assessment *(W, AF2&3)* Can the children write in a formal discussion style with a specific audience in mind?

- Ask the children to write diary entries for Marcus at the end of each chapter.

Assessment *(W, AF2&3)* Can the children use a diary style, combining recount of events with thoughts, opinions and emotions?

Objective Integrate words, images and sounds imaginatively (9.5).

- Ask the children to describe one picture of combat from the story, focussing on precise verbs and adverbs to capture the action.

Assessment *(W, AF7)* Can the children apply appropriate word choices to convey a scene in writing?

Cross-curricular links

Geography/History
- Research other gladiator arenas around the Roman Empire to create an additional Time Out page.

Design & Technology
- Design a new type of gladiator using the information on page 29.

Drama/ICT
- Recreate key scenes via dramatic freeze-framing. Take photos of the freeze-frames and have children add speech and thought bubbles using paper or on screen, creating photo-story versions of the graphic novel.

Lion of Africa

Author: Mary Jennifer Payne

Illustrator: Leo Lingas

Synopsis

A white South African prison guard's view of his country is changed forever when he gets to know the prison's most famous inmate: Nelson Mandela. He leaves the prison service and becomes an anti-apartheid campaigner, and is eventually able to celebrate the release of his inspirational friend.

R, AF = Reading Assessment Focus

W, AF = Writing Assessment Focus

S&L, AF = Speaking and Listening Assessment Focus

C = Language comprehension

V = Vocabulary enrichment

Group or guided reading

Introducing the book

C *(Imagining)* Look at the front cover together. Ask the children, if there are no actual lions in this story, why were the title and cover image chosen?

C *(Predicting)* Ask the children what they think the crowd on the cover are doing. Do they recognise the name on the placard?

C *(Predicting)* Read the blurb together and make predictions about the danger Mandela poses.

C Read the introduction on pages 4 and 5 together to ensure understanding about apartheid and Mandela, then skim through Chapter 1 to check familiarity with the format.

C Look at the characters on page 2. Note real and fictional characters.

C *(Imagining)* Stress the importance of 'reading' the pictures as well as the words, e.g. top of page 9, ask: *How has the artist shown us that John is feeling doubtful?*

C Note the Time Out sections and explain their function as fact pages, informing the reader of the realities and context behind the story.

Strategy Check

V Remind the children to use sounds, familiar words-within-words, sentence and story context *and* the illustrations to make sense of unfamiliar words or phrases.

V *If necessary*, explain 'high treason'.

V Note the glossary on page 48 and model how to use it.

During reading

C *(Deducing)* Ask the children to read Chapter 1, including the Time Out on page 13, and to think about the different opinions of John and Ingrid.

- *(R, AF1)* As the children read independently, listen to each of them in turn, one-to-one, noting and prompting decoding strategies.

Independent Reading

Objective Understand underlying themes, causes and points of view (7.2).

Deducing, Clarifying, Imagining

- Once the children have read Chapter 1, ask them to pair up and discuss briefly Ingrid's attitude to Mandela.
- Discuss John and Ingrid's different opinions about Mandela and apartheid.
- Why does the man on page 11 have to show his pass? What is Ingrid's reaction?
- Look at John's facial expression through the chapter. How does it change at the bottom of page 12?

Assessment Check that the children:

- *(R, AF2)* can summarise Ingrid's view that Mandela is dangerous and that apartheid is good.
- *(R, AF2&3)* understand the inequality of the passbooks and infer Ingrid's hypocrisy regarding this.
- *(R, AF2&3)* can comment on John's doubts about his mother's views.

Returning and responding to the text

Objective Understand underlying themes, causes and points of view (7.2).

Summarising, Clarifying, Deducing, Imagining

- When the children have read the whole story, ask them why Mandela was regarded as dangerous.
- Ask the children to explain why Mandela helped with another man's work in Chapter 2. Why is this important?

- Discuss with the children how John's words and actions on page 40 show that he has learnt from Mandela.
- Look at pages 24–26. How did John feel about his nanny Olivia?
- On page 26, why does Mandela seem to laugh?
- Why is the Time Out on page 37 called 'Worth a Thousand Words'? Why is world opinion important?
- Ask the children to explain how John's daughter, Hope, is named after Mandela.
- Ask the children to evaluate the effectiveness of the Time Out information pages. Which of these was the most powerful?

Assessment Check that the children:
- (R, AF3) can explain white South Africans' fear of Mandela.
- (R, AF2) understand the selflessness that motivates Mandela.
- (R, AF3) can describe the effect of John's affection for his nanny.
- (R, AF6) can comment on the book's purpose of informing readers about Mandela's selfless struggle against inequality.

Speaking and listening activities

Objective Improvise using a range of drama strategies to explore themes (4.1).
- Ask pairs of children to take the roles of John and his mother to improvise a discussion about Mandela's election as president.

Assessment (S&L, AF5) Can the children sustain roles to explore ideas and issues?

Objective Use a range of oral techniques to present persuasive arguments (1.1).

- Organise groups of children to prepare short presentations on South African apartheid for an appropriate audience.

Assessment *(S&L, AF3)* Can the children adapt and vary Standard English with awareness of purpose audience and subject matter?

Writing activities

Objective Select words and language drawing on their knowledge of literary features (9.4).

- Ask the children to write two short diary entries from John's point of view at the end of chapters 2 and 4.

Assessment *(W, AF2&3)* Can the children use a diary style, combining recount of events with thoughts, opinions and emotions?

Objective Establish, balance and maintain viewpoints (9.3).

- Ask the children to write a letter from John to
  a) his nanny, Olivia, after Mandela's release, or
  b) Mandela, in response to the letter on page 41.

Assessment *(W, AF1&2)* Can the children write imaginatively and appropriately from a character's point-of-view?

Cross-curricular links

PHSE/History/ICT

- Further research Mandela's continuing campaigns against inequality.

- Research/present on other Nobel Peace Prize campaigners.

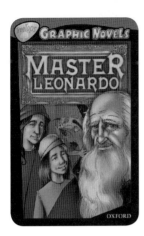

Master Leonardo

Author: Glen Downey & Jayn Arnold

Illustrator: Mike Rooth

Synopsis

Young Matteo is working as the painter Raphael's apprentice when he meets an elderly and disillusioned Leonardo da Vinci. Matteo helps to overcome the rivalries between several Renaissance artists and inspires the old master to paint again. Another of Raphael's workers has a more dangerous grudge, and he plots Leonardo's downfall.

R, AF = Reading Assessment Focus	**C** = Language comprehension
W, AF = Writing Assessment Focus	**V** = Vocabulary enrichment
S&L, AF = Speaking and Listening Assessment Focus	

Group or guided reading

Introducing the book

C *(Imagining)* Look at the front cover together. Ask the children to describe how the younger characters are looking at Leonardo.

C *(Predicting)* Ask them to speculate what is perched on Leonardo's shoulder, and how he came by such a creature.

C *(Predicting)* Read the blurb together and try to speculate why Leonardo would have enemies.

C Skim through Chapter 1 with the children to ensure familiarity with the format.

C Look at the characters on page 2. Note real and fictional people.

C *(Imagining)* Stress the importance of 'reading' the pictures as well as the words, e.g. middle of page 7, ask: *What does the appearance of Leonardo tell us about him at this point?*

C Note the Time Out sections and explain their function as fact pages, informing the reader of the realities and context behind the story.

Strategy Check

V Remind the children to use sounds, familiar words-within-words, sentence and story context *and* the illustrations to make sense of unfamiliar words or phrases.

V Note the glossary on page 48 and model how to use it.

During reading

C *(Deducing)* Ask the children to read Chapter 1 and think about the opinions of Leonardo held by Raphael and Niccolo.

- *(R, AF1)* As the children read independently, listen to each of them in turn, noting and prompting decoding strategies.

Independent Reading

Objective Understand underlying themes, causes and points of view (7.2).

Deducing, Imagining

- Once the children have read Chapter 1, ask them to pair up and discuss briefly the cause of Niccolo's animosity.
- As a group, discuss why Niccolo resents Leonardo, while Raphael – himself a genius painter – admires him.
- On pages 11 and 12, why has the illustrator used copies of Leonardo's frescoes?

Assessment Check that the children:

- *(R, AF3)* can see that Raphael is not threatened by Leonardo's achievements.
- *(R, AF2)* can explain Niccolo's bitterness.

Returning and responding to the text

Objective Understand underlying themes, causes and points of view (7.2).

Summarising, Deducing, Clarifying

- When the children have read the whole story, ask them to discuss the underlying themes of jealousy and resentment.
- Ask the children to explain why Leonardo warms to Matteo on page 16.
- On page 28, why does Matteo say, 'I have seen your work in my master's rooms'.
- How does seeing Raphael's work re-inspire Leonardo?

- Ask children to sum up Michelangelo's character from pages 27 and 40.
- In the children's opinion, what is the greatest work of art presented in this book?
- Ask the children to evaluate the effectiveness of the Time Out information pages. Which of these was the most useful?

Assessment Check that the children:

- (R, AF2) can explain clearly the causes of the various resentments in the story.
- (R, AF2&3) can infer that Leonardo is re-inspired by the younger geniuses.
- (R, AF3) can infer that Leonardo had earlier inspired Raphael and Michelangelo.
- (R, AF6) can comment on the book's purpose of enhancing knowledge of Renaissance art and artists.

Speaking and listening activities

Objective Improvise using a range of drama strategies to explore themes (4.1).

- Hotseat a child as Niccolo, and put him on trial for arson. What reasons for leniency can the child come up with, using evidence from the text? Other children may take roles as prosecution or defence lawyers and witnesses.
- Following research, hotseat a child as Michelangelo and ask him about the experience of painting the Sistine Chapel.
- Play the 'balloon game' with famous artists. Children in role must justify why they should stay in the balloon and the class vote on who gets thrown out!

Assessment **(S&L, AF5)** Can the children sustain roles to explore ideas and issues?

Writing activities

Objective Select words and language drawing on knowledge of formal writing (9.4).

- Following research, ask the children to write a persuasive leaflet for an exhibition of Leonardo's varied work.

Assessment **(W, AF2&3)** Can children use a formal persuasive style, combined with accurate information?

Objective Integrate words, images and sounds imaginatively (9.5).

- Find better reproductions of the works of the three masters. Ask the children to choose one and describe in as much detail as possible, using expanded nouns and adverbial phrases.

Assessment **(W, AF6&7)** Can the children apply appropriate word choices and grammatical accuracy to convey a masterwork in writing?

Cross-curricular links

Art/History
- Undertake further research to create leaflets about Leonardo's legacy. Entitle the leaflets, 'Why are we still talking about Leonardo Da Vinci?'

Art/Thinking skills
- Study one of Leonardo's paintings together and encourage children to think and compose *how, why, when* and *where* questions.

History/Science
- Research more about the *scientific* advances of the Renaissance, including Leonardo's work, for an additional Time Out page.

Riches of the Amazon

Author: Christopher Sweeney

Illustrator: Leigh Dragoon

Synopsis

This is a story about mining company executives trying to move Amazonian Indians from their homes in order to find gold. One of the executives only wants to find the gold; the other is also worried about her epileptic son, Justin. When a tribal shaman gives Justin rainforest medicine, his mother sees another side of the rainforest.

R, AF = Reading Assessment Focus	**C** = Language comprehension
W, AF = Writing Assessment Focus	**V** = Vocabulary enrichment
S&L, AF = Speaking and Listening Assessment Focus	

Group or guided reading

Introducing the book

C *(Predicting)* Look at the front cover together. Ask the children to make predictions about the three people and the green fluid.

C *(Predicting)* Ask the children their ideas on what the 'riches of the Amazon' might be.

C *(Predicting)* Read the blurb together and try to predict what kind of business Justin's mother might have in the rainforest.

C Skim through Chapter 1 with the children to ensure familiarity with the format.

C Look at the characters on page 2. Note real and fictional people.

C *(Imagining)* Stress the importance of 'reading' the pictures as well as the words, e.g. bottom of page 6, ask: *How are the different energy levels of mother and son conveyed?*

C Note the Time Out sections and explain their function as fact pages, informing the reader of the realities and context behind the story.

Strategy Check

V Remind the children to use sounds, familiar words-within-words, sentence and story context *and* the illustrations to make sense of unfamiliar words or phrases.

V Note the glossary on page 48 and model how to use it

During reading

ⓒ *(Deducing)* Ask the children to read Chapter 1 and think about the relationship between Justin and his mother.

● *(R, AF1)* As the children read independently, listen to each of them in turn, noting and prompting decoding strategies.

Independent Reading

Objective Understand underlying themes, causes and points of view (7.2).

Deducing, Clarifying, Imagining

● Once the children have read Chapter 1, ask them to pair up and discuss briefly why Justin becomes cross.

● As a group, recap ways in which Joanna is trying to prevent her son from risk of a seizure. How does Justin respond?

● On page 10, what do Joanna's facial expressions and body language tell us about how she is feeling?

● Ask the children to offer opinions of the relationship between Paolo and Jorge.

Assessment Check that the children:

● *(R, AF2)* understand Justin's annoyance at the interruption to the holiday.

● *(R, AF3)* can see that Joanna is protective of her son, and that Justin wants to be treated normally.

● *(R, AF3)* can infer Jorge's dislike of his boss.

Returning and responding to the text

Objective Understand underlying themes, causes and points of view (7.2).

Clarifying, Summarising, Imagining

- When the children have read the whole story, discuss Joanna's motives for stopping the gold mine: to protect the rainforest or make money from medicines?
- On page 20, can the children explain Joanna's anger with Xu'xulo?
- Look at pages 24–25. Ask the children to explain how Paolo has been made to seem particularly evil.
- Why was Jorge working for Paolo?
- What is the importance of Justin's rainforest tour on pages 32–33?
- Ask the children to evaluate the effectiveness of the Time Out information pages. Which of these was the most interesting?

Assessment Check that the children:

- (R, AF2&3) can identify Joanna's protection of her son.
- (R, AF3) can see that Joanna's business motive is a factor in her new environmentalism.
- (R, AF6) can comment on the book's purpose of persuading us to protect the rainforest.

Speaking and listening activities

Objective *(Improvise)* using a range of drama strategies to explore themes (4.1).

- Hotseat a child as Paolo, putting him on trial for his behaviour. What reasons for mercy can the child consider, using evidence from the text?

Assessment (S&L, AF5) Can the children sustain roles to explore ideas and issues?

Objective Use a range of oral techniques to present persuasive arguments (1.1).

- Following research, ask groups or pairs of children to make persuasive presentations about preserving the rainforest.

Assessment *(S&L, AF3)* Can the children adapt spoken standard English appropriately for subject matter, purpose and audience?

Writing activities

Objective Select words and language drawing on their knowledge of formal writing (9.4).

- Following research, ask the children to write a persuasive leaflet entitled, 'Why the rainforest is important to YOU?'

Assessment *(W, AF2&3)* Can the children use a formal persuasive style, combined with accurate information?

Objective Integrate words, images and sounds imaginatively (9.5).

- Describe Justin's rainforest tour (pages 32–33), using adverbial and expanded noun phrases.

Assessment *(W, AF 6&7)* Can the children apply appropriate word choices and grammatical accuracy to convey the experience?

Cross-curricular links

Geography/Science
- Research rainforest animals and the need to protect habitats to supplement the Wild Time on page 37.

Geography/Science
- Research the impact of deforestation on global warming for an additional Time Out page, posters and presentations.

Geography/Music/Dance/Art
- Compose percussion music and simple costumed dance routines based on research into Rio's Carnival.

First published in 2004 in Great Britain by Gullane Children's Books
This paperback edition published in 2007 by

Gullane Children's Books
an imprint of Alligator Books
Winchester House, 259-269 Old Marylebone Road,
London NW1 5XJ

1 3 5 7 9 10 8 6 4 2

Giselle, Swan Lake, Sleeping Beauty, and *The Nutcracker*
(previously published as individual titles)
Text © Adèle Geras 2000
Illustrations © Emma Chichester Clark 2000

Coppélia and *The Firebird*
Text © Adèle Geras 2004
Illustrations © Emma Chichester Clark 2004

The right of Adèle Geras and Emma Chichester Clark to be identified as the author and illustrator
of this work has been asserted by them in accordance with the Copyright, Designs and Patents Act, 1988.

A CIP record for this title is available from the British Library.

ISBN-13: 978-1-86233-689-6

Printed and bound in China

ADÈLE GERAS & EMMA CHICHESTER CLARK

My First

Ballet Stories

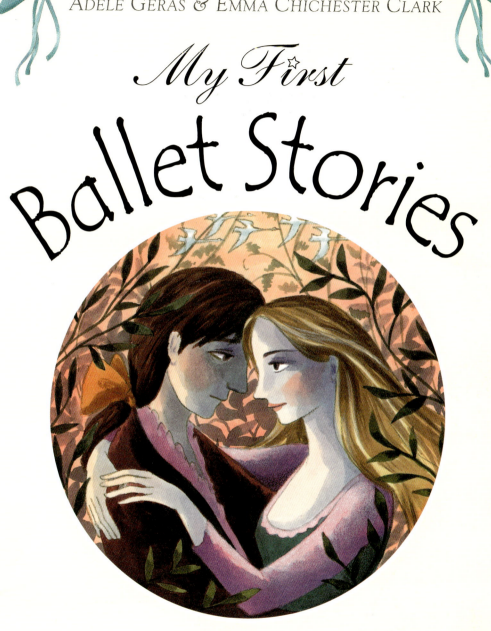

GULLANE
CHILDREN'S BOOKS

Cont

 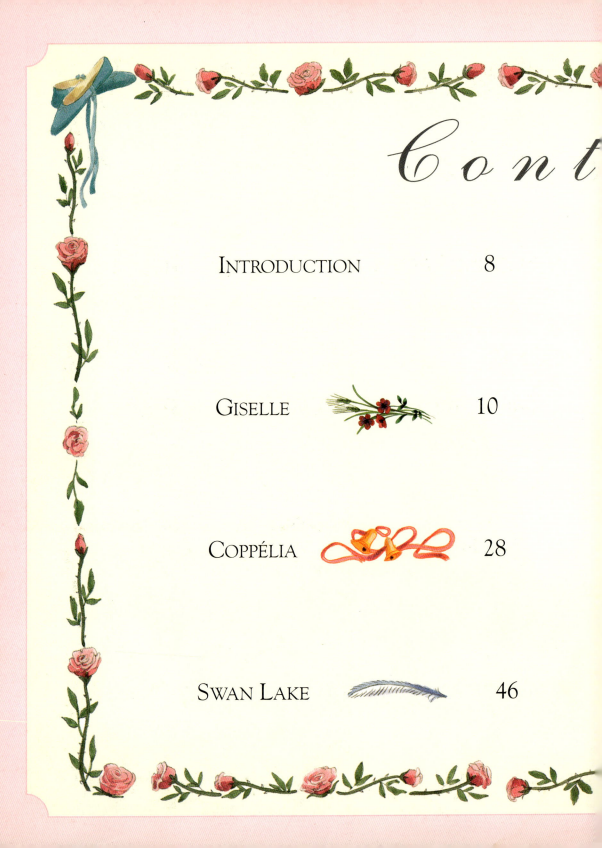

ents

The Magic of the Ballet

HUMAN BEINGS LIKE TO move their bodies in time to rhythm. Even the tiniest babies enjoy being rocked or gently bounced as you sing to them, and we all know how feet long to move when we hear a strong and exciting beat. "That's toe-tapping music," we say, and what we mean is we would like to dance to it.

There are many different kinds of dance: folk, disco, ballroom, tap and so on.

Classical ballet is dancing which follows a very particular set of rules, and some of these go back to the seventeenth century, when such dancing was first seen as a short interlude in the middle of a play, a pleasant break from lines and lines of dialogue. Because there are no spoken words on stage, the same ballets are understood in any country.

The stories behind the ballets are tales of love and transformation, of death and ghosts, of lakes and dark forests and strange creatures. As the curtains open on a ballet, we become part of a magical world and share all its enchantments. We marvel at the grace and discipline of the dancers; at the beauty they create.

'It was Giselle's voice, and I was filled with
a happiness I thought was lost forever.'

Giselle

EVERYTHING THEY SAY ABOUT old age is true. I find that I remember in the clearest detail everything that happened to me in my youth, and yet I would have difficulty in telling you what I ate this morning when I awoke.

Sometimes I forget how quickly the years have gone by and when I catch sight of myself in the glass, I do not recognize the white-haired, old man I see. This cannot be me, Albrecht. Albrecht was tall and straight. He had clear blue eyes and a smiling mouth. And he was loved, oh yes indeed. I may have forgotten many things, but the memory of Giselle's love for me still remains. I think of her every day, and there is a small, vain part of my soul that rejoices to think she never saw me as an old man. To her I am still young.

Giselle lived in the village of . . . but no, the name has gone. No matter. It was a collection of small, well-kept cottages that clung to the side of a hill where the forest ended.

I was hiding in this village, I confess it. I had become bored with palace life, with ceremony, with decorum, and all I wanted that spring was to roam through the woods like a peasant, hunting when it suited me.

It wasn't really even Bathilde I was escaping from. Our families had arranged that we would be married. Bathilde was considered to be a beauty and her father was the Duke of Courland. My parents persuaded me it would be a splendid alliance, and I reluctantly agreed. My flight to the village was a last chance for the kind of freedom I knew I could never have as a married man, nor as the future Duke of Silesia.

If it were not for Giselle, I should probably have returned to the palace within days, but once I caught sight of her, everything else in my life shrank away and I never gave the palace or my duty a single thought. I found a cottage and paid the owner money to rent it, and I took the name of Loys.

How can I find words to describe Giselle? I loved her from the very first moment I laid eyes on her, and she loved me too. She was pale. Her hair was like ravens' feathers. She danced for happiness, but there was always something fragile about her. I don't know how to put it more accurately. Always I had the thought in my mind when we were together, 'be careful, oh, be careful,' for I knew she could so easily be hurt.

Hilarion, the young gamekeeper in the village, adored Giselle too. He could see that Giselle and I loved each other, and his jealousy grew and grew.

On the morning of the harvest feast, I came very near to telling Giselle who I really was.

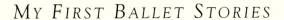

She had been teasing me, asking me why it was that I was different from other men she had known, and begging me to tell her where I had come from and who my family were.

"It doesn't matter," I answered. "You are my family, my whole world. You are the one I love."

"Oh, but do you? Do you truly? Let this flower tell us." She picked a late rose and began idly to pluck the petals from it. "He loves me, he loves me not . . ."
"Will you believe a flower that knows nothing of how I feel? Will you not believe me?"

Suddenly I was filled with dread at what Giselle would do if the last petal fell on 'he loves me not'. How relieved I was then, to pull the last petal from the stem.

the was frind boto

"I love you! You see? Even this rose knows this is the truth!" I cried.

Giselle smiled, happy for the moment.

"Go with the others, Loys, to gather the last of the harvest, and I will stay here and prepare the feast," she said.

And I went. I went gladly. I thought myself the most fortunate man alive, striding away with the others into the valley while the September sun shone all around us, as golden and sparkling as the wine we would soon be enjoying. Try to imagine my joy as a bubble, and look at it now, catching the light. Soon it will burst, and neither I nor anyone else will ever lay eyes on it again.

Much later, during that long, infinitely black night while we watched over Giselle's body before her funeral, her weeping mother told me what had happened. I hear her words even now, half a lifetime later. I still wonder if there was anything I could have done differently that

would have prevented Giselle's dreadful end.

"We heard the horns, and the hounds baying," her mother told me, "and soon a hunting-party arrived in the village. Everyone gathered round, for we had never seen such grand people. Princess Bathilde was the most splendid of all, in a gown the colour of a dark red rose. Everyone was falling over themselves to offer hospitality. Giselle helped to serve the wine, and Princess Bathilde was struck with her beauty and grace."

Here Giselle's mother paused and wiped the tears from her eyes. "Bathilde asked my poor daughter question after question. She begged her to come to the palace as her own serving-lady, but when she found out that Giselle was in love and soon to be married, she smiled kindly.

'It is my loss,' she said, 'and you shall have my own necklace as a wedding-gift.'

She fastened a chain of gold filigree around Giselle's neck and my daughter danced away to

show the wonderful present to all her friends.
The royal party came into my house to rest

before their homeward journey, and then you
came back from the vineyards and the festival
began. My daughter had been chosen as the
Queen of the Harvest. How joyously she
danced! Do you remember? Oh, oh, I cannot
bear to think of what has happened!"

And I, even though I cannot bear it, am
condemned to turn it over constantly in my
mind. I remember how we danced, and then

how Hilarion came rushing from my cottage brandishing my sword. Wine had given Hilarion courage. He parted us, Giselle and me, by placing the blade between us and his face was twisted with hatred.

"You are the son of the Duke of Silesia, and not Loys at all. I have the proof." He turned to the villagers. "He brought too many possessions with him for a humble peasant. He has deceived us, and he has bewitched you, Giselle, with his false promises."

The royal party came out of Giselle's cottage to see what all the shouting was about, and Bathilde caught sight of me at once.

"Albrecht!" she cried, "What are you doing here among these simple folk?" She ran to my side and said, "See, Giselle, I too have my betrothed. This is Albrecht, and I hope that you will be as happy in your marriage as we in ours." And each word was like a dagger in my poor Giselle's heart! Giselle turned to me.

"Please say that she is lying, Loys," she whispered. My mouth was full of ashes, and my heart was as cold as a stone in my body. I could say nothing.

Do you believe that someone can die of a broken heart? I had thought it was a fanciful notion, invented by lovesick poets, but that was before Giselle's death.

She tore at the necklace Bathilde had given her and it snapped as though it were no more than a thin string of silk. Then she took my jewelled sword from Hilarion and plunged it into her side. How could he have let her take it? How could he have prevented her? She had the strength of despair in her hands. Still, it was not the wound that killed her. I did. I killed her as surely as though I had squeezed the life out of her with my own hands. She danced like a marionette with broken strings. She danced like a doll with no life left in her. Her soul flew out of her

before our eyes. The anguish in her heart drove all reason from her and she fell at last into her mother's arms.

The feast was over. No one moved for a long time. Then Balthilde's party left the village. There was nothing they could do. No one was interested in them any longer. We were numb with grief, all of us, and hardly noticed the departure. There was nothing left for us to do but mourn.

"I should throw you from this house," said Giselle's mother, "but my daughter loved you." That was how I came to watch all night over Giselle's body, until her funeral the next day.

Do you believe in Wilis? They are the spirits of young girls who have died before their wedding day, deceived by their lovers, tricked by lies. There were tales told about them by country people. It was said they appeared at midnight, on the swampy shores of a hidden lake, led by their queen, Myrtha, who was tall and white and merciless. The Wilis danced till the first light of dawn, and as the sun's rays touched them, they dissolved, every one of them, into thin mists, stretching and curling and hovering over the water. If an unfortunate young man were to meet one of them in the dark, he would be enchanted by her beauty and she would dance with him, in and out of the black trees in the moonlight, and her white, white arms would wind themselves like smoke

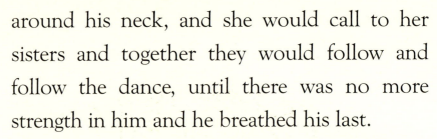

around his neck, and she would call to her sisters and together they would follow and follow the dance, until there was no more strength in him and he breathed his last.

Everyone warned me. "Do not go to Giselle's grave at night. Some say she is now one of Queen Myrtha's misty maidens, and she will dance you to your death."

But I thought, 'If I could see Giselle again, I would gladly pay with my life.' So I said only, "There are flowers I must lay on her grave. Do not try to prevent me."

I knew that there was no one brave enough to stop me as I made my way to where she lay buried.

I threw myself down near the wooden cross carved with Giselle's name. I was beside myself with grief. Then I saw Hilarion slipping through the trees. Could he have arrived before me? The thought flew in and out of my mind like a butterfly and waves of sorrow overwhelmed me.

I laid my face on the cold earth.

"My darling," said a voice near me, and I

knew it. It was Giselle's voice, and I was filled
with a happiness I thought was lost forever. I
looked up, and the blood froze in my veins. It
was indeed Giselle and yet she was transformed.
Her eyes were like black pools and her mouth
was a bloodstain in her chalk-white face.

"Go, my love," she whispered. "I cannot
protect you from your fate if you remain
here. They . . . we will surely lead you to your

grim death. Come quickly with me and I will endeavour to hide you."

I followed her into the darkness between the trees, but at that moment we saw Hilarion dancing with the white maidens. I watched him, pulled this way and that like something blown by the wind, or pulled by the tides, until at last he sank into the waters of the black lake whose surface glittered in the moonlight.

"Look," Giselle whispered. "Our Queen approaches." Queen Myrtha towered over her maidens. Her face was a mask and her dress moved around her like a cloud.

"There is a stranger in our midst," she said. "I can smell him. Giselle, where have you hidden him, the man who drove you to your death? Bring him out to us. We wish for him to dance with us."

Giselle turned to me. "Hold tightly to the cross on my grave," she said. "It is the only thing that will protect you. Do not let go.

Whatever happens, hold tightly onto the cross.
I will plead with our Queen. Perhaps she will
be merciful."

Giselle begged for my life, but Queen Myrtha
was unmoved.

"He will dance," she said, "like all the others.
He will dance until he can dance no longer.
Go to him."

At first, I shut my eyes and clung to the
cross, but I couldn't bear not to see my beloved
when she was so close to me.

"Turn away," she cried. "Hold fast."

But I could not. I had to hold her in my arms
once more. I had to dance with her, even if
death was the punishment.

"No," she whispered. "How will I protect
you if they come . . . all my pale sisters?"

And of course they did come, all the ghostly
dancers, pulling me here and there, making me
feel dizzy and sick.

"Do not fall, my love," Giselle said to me as

we whirled and turned. "Lean on me. I will carry you. Do not lose heart. The light of dawn will soon be here."

As we danced, I lost all thought of where I was and yet I knew that the Wilis were drawing me nearer and nearer to the water. Sometimes I caught sight of it among the trees, but only for an instant, so frantic was the dance. I could feel Giselle breathing cold words of love in my ear.

"Come with me. The dawn is nearly here."

Blindly, nearly exhausted, I followed her. We were very near her grave. I could see the cross I should have clung to, and my own flowers beside it. Then, I caught sight of the sky above the trees. Day was breaking.

"Thank the Lord," Giselle said, "for another dawn. They cannot touch you now. Look."

The Wilis were melting in the light. Even their queen was blurring at the edges and fading away among the trees.

"Stay," I groaned. "Do not leave me here alone, Giselle. What will I do but weep for you?"

"Then weep you shall," she sighed, "for I must return to the grave."

Her shape was disappearing into the earth. Before I could say another word, she was gone. She had saved me with her love and condemned me to a lifetime of remorse and sorrow.

That life is now nearly at an end. I pray that beyond the grave I will be reunited with Giselle. I pray for that.

'There was the 'niece', the beautiful young lady
I had seen sitting on a chair on the balcony.'

Coppélia

THE CELEBRATIONS ARE OVER. The splendid new bell has been hung in the church, and its silver voice sings out over the rooftops, calling the people to prayer. Franz and I are officially engaged. Dr Coppélius has been given a sum of money to repair anything in his house that needs repairing, and also as a kind of apology from the town.

I suppose I am the chief cause of any unhappiness the poor Doctor feels, and for that I am most sincerely sorry. My deception seemed like such harmless fun when I thought of it, and in any case, let us not forget what he did to poor Franz. Let me tell you what happened, and you will judge for yourself.

My name is Swanilda. I have lived in this town all my life and, for as long as anyone

can remember, the tall black house on the market square has belonged to Dr Coppélius. My grandmother tells me that even in her childhood, he never invited anyone into it, nor did he open the windows to let in the daylight. Dr Coppélius must be very old, but he has never looked different from the way he is now. Perhaps he was born grey-haired and stooped and as thin as a skeleton. He makes toys and sells them in the market. There's not a child in the town who has not played with one of his carved dolls or hobby-horses or Jack-in-the-boxes. You would have thought that such a toymaker would be beloved of every child for miles around, but Dr Coppélius was feared by the little ones and ridiculed by the swaggering young men who had grown up on stories of the dark deeds that (according to their nursemaids) took place in the shadowy rooms of the house whose shutters were always closed.

Imagine my astonishment then, when, a few days ago, I saw a most beautiful young lady sitting quite openly on Dr Coppélius's balcony, reading a book.

"Look!" I said to my friends. "That's the first time anyone has ever visited Dr Coppélius. Perhaps it's a relative of his."

I called up to her, in a friendly sort of way, but she didn't even look at me. I thought her proud and stuck-up and decided to leave her reading, if that was what she enjoyed. When I caught a glimpse of Franz coming

into the square, I hid myself at once. I knew he was going to flirt with this total stranger on Dr Coppélius's balcony and that was exactly what he did. I watched him doing it.

It's not that I am particularly jealous by nature, only that Franz and I had already decided that we would be married. We had been keeping company since we were small children, and I loved him dearly. Until I saw him talking to this silent young woman, I would have said he loved me. I gave him a piece of my mind, you may be sure.

"But I was only being friendly," he said. "Aren't you in the slightest bit curious to know who this young lady is? How often have you seen a visitor in that house?"

"Nevertheless," I sniffed. "There's friendliness and friendliness. You are not using the words you would use if you were addressing a toothless old crone. I know you too well, Franz. You think she is prettier than I am.

I don't know if I'm ready to marry someone quite so fickle."

Just then, Dr Coppélius appeared on the balcony, and together, he and the young woman made their way back into the dark house. Franz went about his business, still protesting his undying love for me, and I decided to wait in the square to see what would happen next. Some of my friends were with me. We saw the door of Dr Coppélius's house open, and the old toymaker himself shuffled out, blinking, a little unaccustomed to the bright sunlight. He turned out of the square and made his way down a small cobbled street.

"He's dropped his key on the ground, look!" I said to my friends. "Let's go in and talk to the niece or whoever she may be. No one has ever been into that house. Just think what stories we'll be able to tell. Will you come with me?"

Such terrible tales were told about the Doctor's magic powers that they were fearful at first, but I persuaded them in the end.

"What possible magic can he work," I said, "if he's not even here in the house?"

At last, they agreed to come with me, and we all tiptoed as quietly as we possibly could through the black door. We made our way along gloomy corridors, trying to keep our spirits up by giggling and holding hands. There was no sign of the pretty girl and even though we called out to her as we walked through the house and up the stairs, only silence answered us, a silence so deep that it rang in our ears.

When we reached the upper floor, we found the toymaker's studio. Even I, who had been pretending not to be in the least bit scared, found this room to be a little upsetting. This was the place where Dr Coppélius made his dolls. There were arms and legs hanging from hooks, and blank-faced bald heads propped up on sticks, waiting for wigs. There were glass balls painted to look like real eyes, lying in a tray on one table, and worst of all, there were the finished dolls, who were sitting about the workshop, looking at us through their staring enamelled eyes.

"He is very skilful, to be sure," said my friend Maria. "Look at that mandarin over there, and the knight on his horse."

"I like these two life-sized monkeys in pink

brocade," I said, "and this pretty Spanish dancer. But where is Dr Coppélius's niece?"

"She's not here," said Maria. "Don't you think we'd better go? What if the Doctor comes back and finds us?"

"First just let me quickly see what's in this cupboard," I said.

"What if it's locked?" Maria whispered. It was not locked.

When I opened it, there was the 'niece', the beautiful young lady I had seen sitting on a chair on the balcony. I burst out laughing.

"Franz has been flirting with a doll!" I cried. "Oh, he is bound to feel such a fool when I tell him. Dr Coppélius has tricked us all. He has made a doll so perfect that we all thought she was alive."

I don't know who it was that managed to set the clockwork (or magic, or whatever it was) in motion, but suddenly the whole room was filled with Dr Coppélius's creatures going through their mechanical paces.

"How clever they are!" cried my friends, but I was too busy examining the doll I had found to look at the other toys.

Truly, she was a thing of beauty. I imagined Dr Coppélius working through the long, quiet nights, putting her still limbs together, carefully mixing his paints to the exact colour of flesh that matched my own, sticking down each lock of the hair that was so like mine, touching her long eyelashes with soft brushstrokes. It was easy to see that this was a labour of love.

"We could be sisters," I whispered to her.

Then, all at once, there was the Doctor, shouting at us, flapping his cloak in all directions. My friends were screeching and crying and running round the room and out the door and down the stairs, as fast as their legs could carry them. No one stopped for me, but I was near the cupboard. I didn't think. I simply locked myself in with the doll, and listened as Dr Coppélius soothed his toys, winding them down, stopping their constant movement as gently as any caring father, while he tidied the room. I hid, and waited for a chance to escape, and then I thought of a clever trick I could play on the good Doctor.

Quickly, I undressed the doll, took off my own clothes, and put hers on instead. Then I hid her limp, white body at the back of the cupboard and sat down in her chair, pretending to read her book. I knew it would not be too long before the Doctor came to

make sure that no harm had befallen his most treasured creation.

"There you are, my darling," he crooned. "Safe and untouched. I don't think I could have borne it if any of those silly young girls had harmed you."

Just then there came a tapping at the window. Dr Coppélius turned to see who it was, but I had already spotted Franz, who had clearly climbed a ladder to catch sight of the pretty stranger once more. What a surprise there was in store for him! Dr Coppélius half-closed the cupboard door, and went to the window.

"Welcome, dear sir," he said. "I assume you have come to visit me, even though you have chosen a somewhat unusual way to enter the house. Surely it would have been far simpler for you to knock at the door."

Franz climbed into the room, looking uncomfortable. "I'm sorry, Dr Coppélius,"

he said. "It's just that the young lady . . . well, I did want to see her again, and assure her of my friendship."

"Certainly, young man, certainly," said Dr Coppélius. "See her you shall, but first of all, you will take a little wine with me."

I should have declared myself then, and Franz and I should have run out into the square together, but I was jealous. Franz, it seemed, was interested enough in the young lady to risk breaking into someone's house. I told myself I didn't care what happened to him, but I was wrong. In a few minutes, it became clear that the wine had been drugged and the Doctor was laying my poor Franz out on a table. Then he came and spoke to me.

"There, Coppélia dear. I have drugged him. Now I shall use my best magic to transfer his life force into you."

Of course, I never really believed in any of it: all that nonsense with the spells and the smoke and the way Dr Coppélius waved his bony fingers in the air and hummed to himself . . . and yet, the dolls in his workshop *did* all move in a most intriguing manner. Had they, too, been enchanted? Was it possible? I knew at once what I had to do. My task was to distract him from Franz, and I knew exactly how to do it too. I would come to life, but bit by bit, and he would be so overwhelmed with his own cleverness in creating such a marvel that he would leave poor Franz alone.

My trick worked better than I could have hoped. From jerky wooden movements, I progressed very speedily into such natural gestures that soon I was able to walk about the room quite freely.

"Oh, my beloved Coppélia!" cried the Doctor. "You are wonderous beyond anything I have ever imagined! How full of love I am for you! Dance for me, my beauty. Dance!"

And so I did dance. I danced a Spanish dance, and a Scottish dance and Dr Coppélius was beside himself with pleasure.

Whenever the Doctor wasn't looking, I ran to Franz and shook him and spoke into his ear, and at last, after what seemed to me like hours, he began to stir. I seized my opportunity. I spoke.

"Dr Coppélius, I have to tell you the truth. My name is not Coppélia. It is Swanilda.

Your doll is still lying in the cupboard. I have played a trick on you, and I'm sorry, but this young man is my betrothed, and when I saw that you had drugged him, I was frightened of what you might do to him."

Dr Coppélius gave a cry of horror and rushed to the cupboard. I thought he would shout at us, or threaten us in some way, or chase us from his house, but his thoughts were centred on Coppélia. He carried her floppy white body in his arms, and sank to the ground, weeping.

"Come," said Franz. "Let us go while he isn't looking."

I went with Franz, but I haven't been able to forget the sight: poor, thin, grey Dr Coppélius embracing a lifeless bundle of cloth and kapok and paint in the half-light of the workshop. I could hear him moaning as we left. "I thought you had come to life, my darling. I thought you could dance for me forever. How will I manage now? What will I do?"

The next day was filled with joy and sunshine and feasting. Franz and I agreed to become formally engaged, and we received a handsome dowry from the mayor of the town. I suppose no real harm was done, but I for one will no longer join in any gossip about Dr Coppélius. I feel sorry for him, because, even though he has been compensated for the damage we did in his house, all the money in the world will

never buy him a living companion, and
loneliness must be the very iciest of sorrows.
I am the only person in the town who truly
knows Dr Coppélius, for I was his Coppélia
for a while, and I felt the warmth and
tenderness of his love.

'Von Rothbart swooped down from his branch and the
black span of his wings obscured the moon.'

Swan Lake

LISTEN. THESE THINGS HAPPENED long ago. There was daylight and darkness. There was Good and Evil. There was the kingdom and the forest. In the kingdom, Prince Siegfried was about to celebrate his birthday. The forest, however, was the lair of the magician, Von Rothbart.

In the deepest and greenest part of the forest, there was a silver lake which people called 'The Lake of Swans'. Whispers were that every bird floating on the still waters was really a young maiden trapped by Von Rothbart and transformed into a swan for as long as there was light in the sky.

At dusk, (so the story went) each bird took on her human shape for the length of the night, and in this way, Von Rothbart would remind them of the human happiness they had lost. Every single night, the magician took on the feathers and talons and wide amber eyes of an enormous owl, and he sat and watched the pale dancers from the branches of a tree beside the lake. The most magnificent swan of all was once a princess. As the sun set, and her feathered wings fluttered into arms, she would remember her name.

"I was Odette," she would sigh. "Once, I was Odette."

But listen. It was the day of Prince Siegfried's birthday, and in the palace, everyone was preparing for the celebrations.

The Queen had planned a ball, and every eligible young lady from every neighbouring country had been invited.

"It is time," the Queen told her son, "that you found yourself a wife. There is a limit to the time a young man of royal birth should spend in frivolous pursuits such as hunting."

"Then why, dearest Mother, did you present me with this crossbow as a birthday gift?" replied the Prince.

"Because I knew it would please you," said the Queen. "In return, I insist that you please me and choose a wife at the ball tomorrow night."

"Very well, Mother," said Prince Siegfried. "You know I would do anything to bring a smile to your lips. Until the ball,

however, I am a free man and I'll enjoy my 'frivolous pursuits', as you call them, for a little while longer."

Siegfried looked out of the window, thinking that perhaps it was too late to go hunting that day. Just then, however, a formation of white swans crossed the sky, making for the dense forest.

"Come," Siegfried called to his companions, "we may be too late, but how beautiful they are! Let's follow them."

The hunting party set off. Although the young men had heard stories about the foolishness of wandering through the forest at dusk, they put them out of their minds. Were they not armed? And what royal prince would ever admit that he was afraid? Nevertheless, as the shadows

thickened and the sky grew dark, Prince
Siegfried's friends urged him to return to
the safety of the palace.

"Wait," said Siegfried. "Can you see
something white moving through the
branches? I'm going to look."

He arrived at the clearing beside the lake
in time to watch the great, white birds that
he had been hunting fly down to the
ground. He raised his crossbow to his

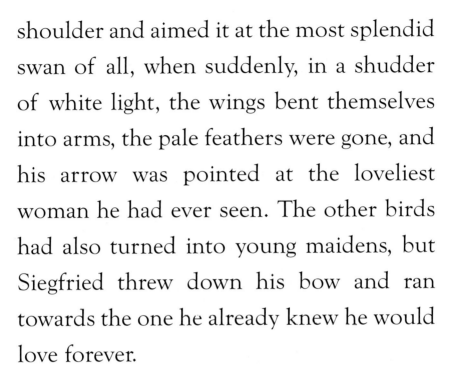

shoulder and aimed it at the most splendid swan of all, when suddenly, in a shudder of white light, the wings bent themselves into arms, the pale feathers were gone, and his arrow was pointed at the loveliest woman he had ever seen. The other birds had also turned into young maidens, but Siegfried threw down his bow and ran towards the one he already knew he would love forever.

"Please," he implored, as she tried to escape him. "Please, I will never hurt you, I promise. Please do not run from me."

In his nearby tree, Von Rothbart, in the guise of an owl, hooted and spread his dark wings, but Siegfried had eyes and ears only for the woman before him.

When he caught up with her, she

trembled in his arms as though she were still a bird and he a hunter, but his kind words soothed her in the end, and she spoke her name aloud to him.

"I am the Princess Odette," she said, "and I am condemned to be a swan during the daylight hours. We are all of us in Von Rothbart's power, and at night we dance in human form, but he watches us always. Even now, his eyes are fixed on us."

"Where?" cried Siegfried. "Show him to me and I will put a single arrow through his heart."

"Oh, no, you must not!" cried Odette, "for then you will surely kill me. He has bound his life to mine and twisted them together in a single thread. If he dies, then so do I. The spell will be broken only

when I can find the person who will love me forever. Someone who will be faithful to me alone."

"Then you are free," Siegfried laughed, "for I shall love you through this life and beyond it. Come with me and be my bride."

Hearing these words, Von Rothbart swooped down from his branch and the black span of his wings obscured the moon. He clawed Odette to his side.

"Go!" said Odette. "There is nothing you can do. The dawn is nearly here and we shall all be swans again."

"I will come back for you," Siegfried cried. "I will find a way to break the spell."

"But go now," Odette sighed. "Only your faithful love can free me from this terror."

All through the next day, the day of the ball, Siegfried was in a dream of love and sorrow. How could he tell his mother that he had found his bride? How could he bring Odette to the palace when Von Rothbart watched and watched her with his amber eyes?

When the ball began, and all the princesses were paraded before him, Siegfried hardly noticed them. Then there came a knocking at the gates.

"Lady," said a messenger, kneeling before the Queen, "a knight and his daughter have arrived and they beg to enter."

"Let them in," said the Queen. "All are welcome at this feast."

The knight was dressed from head to foot in black. Something about his face, and the yellowish light that shone from his eyes seemed familiar to Siegfried, but then he caught sight of the knight's daughter, and recognized Odette, dressed in glittering black. So happy was he to see his swan-lady again that he forgot every other thought in his head and never considered how his beloved had come to be here, at the palace.

All through his life, the prince had learned nothing about deception. Even the

presence of the black knight did not arouse his suspicions, but the princess, although she had the body and face of Odette, was none other than Odile, Von Rothbart's daughter. Her father had given her the outward appearance of Odette for one reason and one reason alone: to entrance and delude poor Prince Siegfried, who would thus be tricked into breaking his faith with his true love.

And oh, this Odile, how she danced and turned, and turned and smiled and how

soft were the fires that shone from her eyes, binding Siegfried's heart to her, and pushing out of his mind every lingering memory of the real Odette's white dress and her gentle beauty.

They danced together in the light of a thousand candles, but Von Rothbart was always near, weaving stronger and stronger enchantment around them. And as they danced, at the high windows of the Great Hall there was a movement . . . a tremble of white at the glass, but no one saw it, and no one heard the frantic arms beating against the pane.

Von Rothbart spoke at last to Siegfried. "If you will promise to love my daughter forever, she shall be yours."

And the Prince (but where, where had he

seen eyes like that before, and why did the knight's black cloak remind him of wings?) spoke the words Von Rothbart was waiting to hear.

"I shall love her, and no one else, for the rest of my days. She is the bride that I have chosen."

A terrible cry came from somewhere high up. Prince Siegfried glanced at the window, and saw the bird-shape of Odette pushing at the glass: desperate, despairing.

The instant he looked back at the knight in black, he knew him to be Von Rothbart. And the young woman at his side? How could he, even for a single moment, have thought that she was his princess? And how could he save Odette,

now that he had broken his promise to her? Siegfried fled from the Great Hall and ran out into the night. He had to find Odette at the lake, and convince her of his love.

At the palace, the guests hurried to leave the ball. The candles flickered and guttered into darkness, and Von Rothbart and his daughter vanished into the night.

Beside the lake, Prince Siegfried found

his princess, weeping and heartbroken. Over and over again he pleaded with her: "I thought that she was you. Oh, the wickedness of that cursed magician!"

"The spell will never be broken for me now," said Odette, "but if I die, then he dies too. Our lives, his and mine, are twisted into a single thread. What can I live for now?"

"If you are gone," said Siegfried, "life has no meaning for me."

"Then let us die together," said Odette.

At that moment, black wings covered the moon, and Von Rothbart swooped down, desperately trying to pull Odette away from Siegfried.

Siegfried and Von Rothbart struggled and fought, and at last the prince broke free of the talons and the beak. Taking Odette's hand, he ran towards the lake. A wind had sprung up, whipping the water into waves and whirlpools. The lovers flung themselves in, sinking deeper and deeper until all became silent and calm once again. Von Rothbart flew into the green heart of the forest to die.

Now the swan maidens were free but they wept bitterly for their princess and her love, together at last.

Listen. These things happened long ago. There is a lake in the forest to this day, but the swans are real swans now. Love, which is stronger than death and lasts forever, has destroyed an evil magic.

On nights when the moon is full, some say they have seen shadows that could be

the Princess Odette and her prince,
dancing beside the silver water of a lake.
A lake they call the Lake of Swans.

'Tiny droplets of blood had stained her dress.'

Sleeping Beauty

MY NAME IS CARABOSSE. People call me all sorts of things. The Bad Fairy, the Wicked Fairy, or the Black Fairy are the most common, but Carabosse is what I prefer. I am old. I am the oldest fairy in the kingdom, and for this reason, if for no other, you would think that King Florestan and his wife would have seen to it that I received an invitation for what promised to be quite the most glittering event in the social calendar: the christening of their longed-for baby daughter, Aurora. They thought (and this is their excuse and it is too feeble to be anything but an excuse) that I had retired. Invitation or not, I went anyway.

"No one had seen you," King Florestan told me at the party, "for ages and ages, and we all thought you had retired, or emigrated."

"Quite the reverse," I said. I was enjoying his embarrassment. In fact, once I had made my entrance, I was determined to enjoy the whole party as much as possible. The best thing of all was the surprise and dismay I caused as I arrived at the door. No one was expecting me.

The entire palace staff had been running about for hours, laying on enough food to feed an army, polishing the wooden floors, dusting down the chandeliers, and wreathing marble columns with garlands of roses. I had seen them in my magic mirror. I'd been watching them for days, and they'd known nothing about it.

At first I thought that I would leave them to get on with the celebrations, but when I saw them gathering near the cradle, oohing and aahing and behaving in a thoroughly silly fashion, I decided to punish them. I was in a very bad temper that day, I admit. I decided, in the blink of an eye, that Princess Aurora would have to perish. That would wipe the smile off their faces, oh yes indeed! What a lesson it would be for King Florestan and the Queen! How dare they invite the others and leave me out?

By the time I reached the palace, (having tossed a few thunderbolts and lightning flashes out of the coach as I passed over the garden, just to announce myself) the other fairies had already given Princess Aurora their gifts. These were exactly the sort of thing I had come to expect from my predictable relations: Joy, Beauty, Intelligence and so forth. Naturally, all the present-giving stopped as soon as I stepped into the room. That was when poor Florestan started mumbling his excuses, but I wasn't interested in listening to him. I went straight to the cradle and said, "I have a gift for the Princess Aurora. Sixteen years of happiness and beauty. And after that, I'm afraid, she will prick her finger on a spindle and drop down dead."

Then I flung myself into my black coach.

"Fly!" I said to the moths that pulled it along. "Fly away. We are not wanted here."

I did feel a great deal better after that, but not for long. When I looked into my magic mirror to see what the effect of my announcement was, I discovered that the Lilac Fairy had not yet bestowed her gift. There she was, right before my eyes, busy undoing some of my magic. How dare she!

"Princess Aurora will not die," she was saying, "but sleep for a hundred years until she is woken by a prince's kiss."

I was angrier than ever. What good to me was a hundred-year sleep? Kisses from a handsome prince were no part of my plan. I was seething with rage. I went to bed that night vowing to outwit the Lilac Fairy even if it took me sixteen years to do it. How dare she pit her puny powers against me, the wicked fairy Carabosse? I became more determined than ever that the Princess Aurora would not have her life for very long. I would attend to it, even if it were the last thing I ever did.

I, the Lilac Fairy, don't like to speak unkindly of anyone, but I make an exception when it comes to Carabosse. She is so wicked, evil and ugly that whatever one says about her can never be too harsh.

Still, the way Carabosse behaved at poor Princess Aurora's christening shocked us all. It was the purest good luck that I had not yet given the baby my gift and so I was able to soften the ill-wishing just a little.

It's done now. Sixteen years we have waited and now the waiting is over. Princess Aurora

is asleep in her chamber, with King Florestan and his Queen on comfortable chairs nearby. I have enchanted everyone, and every living thing from the footmen, fast asleep in the corridor, to the cat curled up by the cold fireside. They will not wake for one hundred years. It is very quiet in the palace now. There will be only dust, gathering on the surfaces of things, because the spiders are asleep and can spin no webs at all. I shall raise a forest of thorns and brambles around the building to shield it from sight until the right person comes to break the spell. It is strange to remember that until a few hours ago we had begun to believe that all would be well.

King Florestan banned spindles from his kingdom within minutes of Carabosse's pronouncement. The very next day, there was a bonfire in the market square, and people came from the furthest corners of the

land to throw their spindles into the flames. How the fire leapt and roared and how we rejoiced to see that everything that could possibly threaten Princess Aurora was being reduced to ashes.

Then the years slid by, faster than anyone could have imagined, and before we knew where we were, it was the Princess' sixteenth birthday. One of my sisters had bestowed on her the gift of beauty, and in her birthday dress she was as lovely as a rosebud. Every rose in the palace garden had bloomed in her honour and there were garlands everywhere. Four young princes from neighbouring territories had come to offer themselves as suitors for her hand, and although she danced with them in the most delightful way possible, I could see that she would love none of these. Do not ask me how. It is simply my duty as a fairy to know such things, just as I knew that whatever the King and Queen thought, the danger from Carabosse was still something to be reckoned with.

Still, even I, intoxicated with joy and sunshine and the fragrance of the roses, let my guard slip a little. I should have been more careful, more vigilant. I shall never cease to blame myself.

A crowd gathered to wish the Princess well. One old lady hobbled up to her with a pretty bunch of flowers. It would have been difficult to refuse such an offering. Princess Aurora took it and thanked the old lady kindly. As the old crone shuffled slowly away into the crowd, something about her seemed to remind me of Carabosse. I would have spoken, but all eyes were on Aurora. She, it seemed, had pricked herself on a thorn. Perhaps the roses in the bouquet had not been carefully trimmed. In any case, she had fainted from the shock, and tiny droplets of blood had stained her dress.

Just then the old lady threw back her hood and cackled, "Oh, look at you all! Fools! Did you think you could defeat me? Idiots! I am Carabosse, and there, in the flowers you will find hidden a spindle. So much for your precious Princess Aurora!"

She flapped her black cloak about her and vanished in a puff of foul-smelling smoke. I took charge at once.

"Bring the Princess to her bedchamber. It has come to pass exactly as I predicted. Let everyone who does not live in the palace leave instantly. We have miracles to perform."

Everyone left the garden. Princess Aurora was carried to her bed and the rest was easy.

Now they are all sleeping. The forest of briars and thorns is growing even as I speak. Princess Aurora is safe. I, the Lilac Fairy, will guard her for the next hundred years, until the spell is broken. A hundred years is but the twinkling of an eye for me. It will pass.

❧❦❧

This has been the strangest day's hunting I've ever had. I set out to find deer and I found – well, let me tell you the story.

My name is Florimund. I am a prince of the royal blood. We, my companions and I, had decided to explore the hills and valleys beyond our own borders, and that was how we found ourselves in a forest that I had never seen before. There were no proper trees in this place, only towering brambles and thickets of wild roses. My hunting party grew nervous and begged me to turn back, but I was fascinated by this place.

"You go," I said, "and I will come after you later. I wish to find what is hidden in the heart of this prickly maze."

So they left me and the silence all around filled my ears. The daylight was fading.

You can imagine how astonished I was, then, when five beautiful ladies suddenly appeared

before me. Their leader, covered in a lilac cloak, stepped forward.

"Do not be afraid, Prince Florimund," she said as she looked into my eyes.

"How do you know my name?" I asked.

"I know very many things," she answered. "I know, for instance, who your true love will be. She is closer than you know."

I smiled at this. If she knew everything, how could she not know that I already had my eye on Valentina, the fairest maid in my kingdom?

"I am already in love," I said.

"That is what you think," whispered the lady in the lilac cloak. "But look first at Princess Aurora. Look first, and then tell me that you love another."

I peered through the trees, and there was the most beautiful lady I had ever seen. She glided between the dark branches like a ghost. I moved towards her. She said nothing, only danced with me. Her beauty bewitched me. Then, as quickly as she had appeared, she vanished into the shadows.

"That," said the lady in lilac, "was but a vision of the Princess. The real person is even lovelier. She has been asleep in a palace in the depths of this wood for a hundred years, but she is waiting for someone who loves her to wake her from her long slumber."

"How can I find her?" I cried. "Show me how to find her!"

For of course the Lilac Fairy was right and

I had lost my heart entirely.

"Cut down these thorns," she said to me, "and you will find your heart's desire."

She slipped away into the darkness, followed by her companions, and I was all alone. I unsheathed my sword and began to make my way through the tangled branches, cutting and slashing at anything that blocked my path. Thorns tore at the skin of my hands and face. Sharp twigs snatched at my garments. I do not know how long I spent in the forest, but after what seemed like hours, I caught sight of the white walls of the palace, glimmering in the moonlight.

I should have known that the Forces of Darkness would be lying in wait for me. I was attacked by huge, black moth-shapes, and bat-shapes, and a hideous crone with a stick and cloak, but I laid about me with my sword and drove them back into the shadows.

"Go," I shouted, "you are evil creatures

and I want nothing to do with you! Nothing is more powerful than my love."

After their shrieks had died away, I made my way into the echoing hall of the palace. Everywhere I looked, people were lying fast asleep, grey under a thick blanket of dust. The Princess, lying on her bed, had been protected by the gauzy bed-curtains. It seemed to me that she had closed her eyes only a moment ago. As soon as I saw her, I knew that I would never love another, and that Princess Aurora would be my bride. I bent over and kissed her. She stirred and opened her eyes. All around us, the palace slowly came to life, but I was unaware of it. I had broken the spell that had bewitched the princess, but now I was enchanted in turn.

I said, "When I set out for the hunt this morning, I never dreamed that you were what I would find."

Princess Aurora smiled.

I am Aurora, bride of Prince Florimund, and my wedding party is over. Tomorrow we will set out for his home and I shall see my new kingdom. I shall miss my godmothers, the fairies, but I shall especially miss the Lilac Fairy. It is thanks to her that Carabosse has at last fled from this land and will worry us no longer. I am grateful to the Lilac Fairy for many things. She looked after me and kept me from the dangers that have beset me since the day I was born. I shall miss my parents and my home, but shall take with me happy memories of my wedding day ball.

"Who would you like," the Lilac Fairy asked, "to dance at your party?"

I was feeling whimsical, I suppose. I said,

"I would like Red Riding Hood and the Wolf, Puss-in-Boots and the White Cat, and of course the Bluebird of Happiness."

So my beloved Lilac Fairy worked her magic once again, and there they were, dancing and feasting with all the other guests. Tonight, when I close my eyes, I know that I will wake up in the morning and look into the face of my darling Florimund. The nightmares that filled my head for a hundred years, of black thorns and matted branches, are gone forever, and I shall have nothing but sweet dreams from now on.

'Snowflakes, enormous and intricately patterned,
circled all about us.'

The Nutcracker

"DREAMS," WHISPERED A DISTANT voice in Clara's ear, "are strange and wonderful things, and dreams that are dreamed on Christmas Eve are the strangest and most wonderful of all."

Clara opened her eyes. There was the china cabinet, and the fireplace, and there in the corner was the Christmas tree. This was most definitely the parlour. Why was she lying on the scratchy plush of the sofa? Why was she not in her own bed, waking up to look for her stocking full of nuts and oranges and twists of golden barley sugar? Clara turned her head and caught sight of the present Dr Drosselmeyer had given her last night at the party: a wooden nutcracker in the shape of a man. Clara picked him up and cuddled him.

"I love you best, Nutcracker," she said. "Better than my dolls. Better than any game. Better than all my other presents. Do you remember being in my dream last night? Do you remember how it all started? I do."

Clara sat up and gathered the travelling rug more closely round her shoulders.

"Now I shall tell you the whole story, Nutcracker," Clara said. "Sit comfortably on this cushion and I'll go right back to the beginning of our party."

The nutcracker said nothing, but he seemed content to listen, so Clara continued. "We always have a party, every year on Christmas Eve. Everyone comes to it: grandfathers and grandmothers, aunts, uncles, cousins, friends and neighbours and Dr Drosselmeyer. Dr Drosselmeyer is not a relation and he's not really a friend but he always comes to the house on Christmas Eve and brings the most marvellous presents.

The preparations for the party were almost as exciting as the party itself. All day long, the house had been full of the most mouth-watering smells, and at last Mama began to set out the food on the long table.

'If you children help with the cakes and sweets,' Mama said, 'there will be none left for the guests! Go instead and fetch your Papa and decorate the tree.'

That's what we did, Nutcracker, and oh, when we'd finished, it was the most beautiful Christmas tree in the whole world. We tied red ribbons on the branches. We hung up painted pine cones, and gingerbread biscuits iced in pink and white, and chocolate coins in glittery paper, and Papa found a silver star for the very top of the tree.

As for the food, you cannot imagine how delicious it was. There were cinnamon biscuits and golden shortbread and animals made out of marzipan. There were tiny crystallised fruits, and sugared almonds and salted almonds, and every cake you can think of: ginger cakes and chocolate ones, and apple cakes and sponges, all set out on dainty china plates patterned with flowers, ivy leaves and trailing ribbons.

The snow started falling at about four o'clock. Fritz and I watched it from our nursery window as it fell from the dark sky, dancing and whirling as the wind lifted it and tossed it over the rooftops, but always in the end falling and falling until everything we could see was covered in white.

'Just like the icing on one of the cakes downstairs,' said Fritz.

When the guests came into the house, snowflakes came in with them: on their hats and capes, on their gloves and boots, and they shook them off, laughing.

'Dr Drosselmeyer is here!' Fritz cried and we both went into the hall to greet him.

'Good evening, children,' he said in his gravelly voice. 'Come and see who I have brought to your party.'

Standing behind him in the shadows were a pretty young lady and a young man wearing a harlequin costume.

'I have taken the liberty of inviting the real Harlequin and Columbine to the festivities.' He put a skinny finger to his lips and whispered to us, 'They are dancing dolls, my

dears, nothing more. Lifesize and very convincing, but only dolls, when all is said and done. Let us see if we can play a trick on the grown-ups.'

And they believed him, Nutcracker. Everyone believed him. Harlequin and Columbine danced for all the guests, and everyone thought they were real. When the dance was over and the secret a secret no longer, all the children clustered round the dolls, touching their stiff limbs that only a moment ago had been so full of life and movement.

Then, Dr Drosselmeyer gave us our presents. There was a set of soldiers in a wooden box for Fritz and you were my gift. Oh, I was delighted with you, and everyone admired you greatly. During the parlour games and dances, I never let you out of my sight, and when Fritz and the other boys took you and began cracking nuts with you, why, I nearly burst into tears. I did cry when they broke you. Anyone would have. How could they have given you such an enormous nut? It would have broken the strongest nutcracker in the world. Dr Drosselmeyer noticed my tears.

'Do not cry, Clara. This is a prince among nutcrackers, and see, a twist here and a turn there and he is as good as new.' The doctor's bony, white hands moved so fast that I could not see what he did, but you were quite mended when he returned you to me.

The end of a party is a sad time, Nutcracker, isn't it? All the candles on the

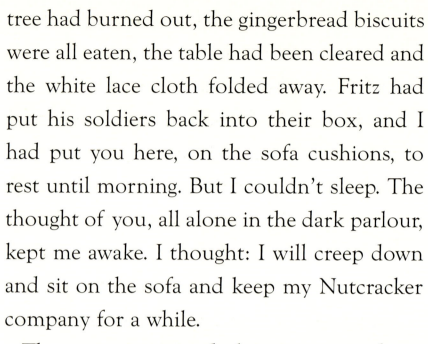

tree had burned out, the gingerbread biscuits were all eaten, the table had been cleared and the white lace cloth folded away. Fritz had put his soldiers back into their box, and I had put you here, on the sofa cushions, to rest until morning. But I couldn't sleep. The thought of you, all alone in the dark parlour, kept me awake. I thought: I will creep down and sit on the sofa and keep my Nutcracker company for a while.

The room was in darkness, except for a faint glow from the embers in the fireplace. I tiptoed to the sofa and sat holding you in my hand. From a long way away, I heard the town clock chiming midnight. Suddenly, the Christmas tree, standing like a shadow in the corner, began to grow. It grew and grew, up and up towards the ceiling with a rustling and creaking and sighing of the branches, and as it grew, the candles seemed to be alight once again, and in a few moments, the tree was towering high, high above my head. Now I know I must have been dreaming, but last night I thought there was a special Christmas magic in the air, for all at once, you and I were the same size and I didn't even stop to consider how strange this was. Then, in the silence of the night, we heard a scratching and a squeaking from behind the Christmas tree.

'It's the Army of Mice,' you said. Yes, you could speak and it seemed to me altogether normal that you should. 'They have come to do battle with the toy soldiers.'

I could hardly believe my eyes. The mice and the soldiers were enormous. They were the same size as we were, and some were even larger. Our Turkish carpet was turned into a battlefield, with Fritz's army waving their swords and shooting their cannons and marching towards their enemy.

You, my brave Nutcracker, decided to attack the Mouse King, a fearsome iron-grey

creature with glittering red eyes.

'Nutcracker!' I cried, afraid. 'He will break you . . . I cannot let you be broken again!'

Suddenly, I was no longer frightened. Instead, I was filled with anger. I took off my slippers and threw them, as hard as I could, at the Mouse King. Perhaps I was helped by Christmas magic once more, for both slippers hit the Mouse King full in the face. He was not expecting slippers to come flying through the air, and he ran away squealing into the shadows under the sideboard. His Mouse Army followed him and soon the soldiers were marching triumphantly back to their box.

'Thank you, Clara,' you said to me. 'You saved my life.'

When I turned to look at you, you were no longer made of wood. You had become a real person, living and breathing . . . a handsome prince. Then you took my hand and we came to sit together on this sofa.

'Your kindness deserves a reward,' you said. 'Close your eyes and do not open them until I tell you to.'

I closed my eyes and felt the sofa moving. It seemed to me that I was flying up and up. I could feel a breeze around us, but I wasn't cold, in spite of being dressed only in my nightgown.

'Open your eyes, Clara,' you said to me. 'We are in the Land of Snowflakes.'

There was nothing in the Land of Snowflakes but clear, dark blue everywhere: above, below and all around us. The sofa was floating on it, through the velvety night. Snowflakes,

enormous and intricately patterned, circled all about us like white moths, floating and drifting, falling and turning.

'They are dancing, Clara,' you told me. 'They are dancing a Snowflake Waltz.'

And indeed, when I looked at them more closely, I could see that this was so. Round and round they twirled, like pretty ladies in white dresses, round and round to a music that grew out of the blue night and swelled around us.

'Come,' you said, when the last snowflake had blown away. 'Now it is time to go somewhere altogether warmer.'

'Where?' I asked. 'Where are we going now?'

'To a party in the Land of Sweets.'

'I have never heard of such a land. When will we reach it?'

'Soon,' you answered. 'Soon. We must hurry. The Sugar Plum Fairy is waiting for us in her palace.'

Now everyone has heard of the witch's house in the story of Hansel and Gretel – the one that was made of things to eat – and I think I was expecting something like that. But I could not have imagined anything half as splendid as the palace of the Sugar Plum Fairy. It was gigantic, and made entirely of pink sugar, spun into domes and turrets and battlements. It was set in a garden full of caramels, marzipan rosebushes, nut-cakes, raisins and pistachios, arranged in tubs and in flowerbeds. The sentries were silver-coated chocolate soldiers.

We went up the flight of steps to the front door, and stepped inside. The walls of every room in the palace were studded with boiled sweets like jewels and the vases were filled with lollipops instead of flowers.

Then, the Sugar Plum Fairy appeared.

'Welcome, Prince Nutcracker, and welcome, Clara, to the Land of Sweets. All that is delicious is waiting for you here.'

Her pink dress caught the light as though she had been sprinkled from head to toe with grains of the finest sugar.

'When you have eaten and drunk, my

friends,' said the Sugar Plum Fairy, 'we will make music, and dance for you.'

The lamps were lit, and fountains sprang to life. Do you remember all the dances, Nutcracker? There was one in honour of chocolate, with all the dancers in Spanish costumes, then one for coffee, with the dancers dressed in veils and richly-patterned Arabian robes. And did you notice the dragons embroidered on the jackets of the Chinese dancers, who represented tea? Oh, they were magnificent. Then came the Russian dancers, with high leather boots and fur hats, and dancers pretending to be reed flutes, and best of all was a huge old lady with a wide, wide skirt under which were hidden dozens and dozens of children.

'Who's that?' I asked, and the Sugar Plum Fairy answered, 'She has many names. Some people call her Mother Ginger or Mother Marshmallow, or even the Old Woman who

Lived in a Shoe, but I call her Mère Gigogne.'

Mère Gigogne and her children stepped aside, the Waltz of the Flowers began, and then, do you remember, Nutcracker? You danced with the Sugar Plum Fairy. To me it seemed as though her feet never touched the ground. You looked so beautiful, both of you. I have never seen a lovelier sight.

There's always a dance at the end of every party, but in the Land of Sweets the last waltz was like a kaleidoscope of sparkling colours, turning and turning.

After the party was over, you and I, Nutcracker, went back into the garden of the palace, and sat down again on our sofa.

'It is time for you to leave us,' said the Sugar Plum Fairy as she bent to kiss me goodbye. 'Take a little rose from this marzipan rosebush.' She put into my hand a pink flower nestling among leaves of green angelica.

'Thank you,' I said. 'It has been like a dream.'

'Dreams,' said the Sugar Plum Fairy, 'are strange and wonderful things, and the dreams that are dreamed on Christmas Eve are the strangest and most wonderful of all.'

That's what she said to me, Nutcracker. Then I woke up. There was a rug covering me. Mama must have come in and found me asleep. Wasn't that a lovely dream, Nutcracker?"

Clara listened for the nutcracker's answer, but he only smiled and said nothing.

Unnoticed under the sofa, a small pink marzipan rose, nestling among green angelica leaves, lay where it had fallen.

'Prince Ivan followed the Firebird, and as she fluttered to
the ground, he stalked her silently as any cat.'

The Firebird

LONG, LONG AGO AND far, far away over the grey looming mountains, in a place where the trees grow tall and dark, and the wolves still howl by moonlight, there lived (so the old stories tell us) a sorcerer whose name was Kostchei.

His palace was set in a garden filled with magic, and travellers told of an orchard where golden apples grew on an enchanted tree. Kostchei was immortal, as long as his soul was kept separate from his body. So he kept it locked up in an egg encrusted with moonstones and rubies, and he kept this egg well-hidden, for no one could kill him if his soul was safely guarded.

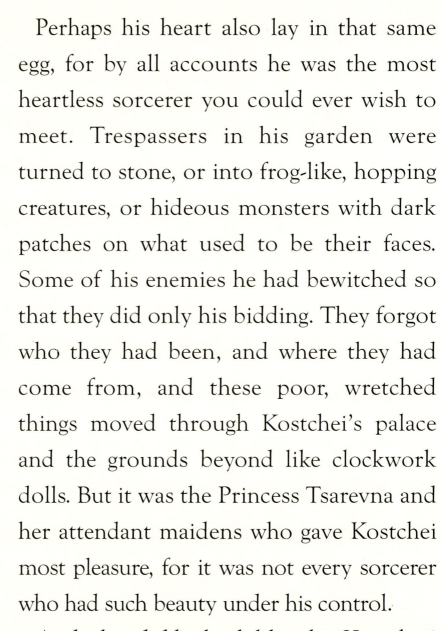

Perhaps his heart also lay in that same egg, for by all accounts he was the most heartless sorcerer you could ever wish to meet. Trespassers in his garden were turned to stone, or into frog-like, hopping creatures, or hideous monsters with dark patches on what used to be their faces. Some of his enemies he had bewitched so that they did only his bidding. They forgot who they had been, and where they had come from, and these poor, wretched things moved through Kostchei's palace and the grounds beyond like clockwork dolls. But it was the Princess Tsarevna and her attendant maidens who gave Kostchei most pleasure, for it was not every sorcerer who had such beauty under his control.

And what did he look like, this Kostchei? Like your very worst nightmares, my children: dark as shadows, tall as towers, and pale as dead men's bones. As for his hands . . . his nails were as long and silvery as knives and his voice was as cold as the winds blown down from the Arctic Circle.

Do you feel cold, my children? Gather round the fire, close to me, and I will tell you how the evil Kostchei was defeated. Look into the grate and tell me what you see. Scarlet and sparkling gold, yes indeed. Something that leaps and glows and dances like a living creature made of light and heat: the fire itself. But look closer. See how the shapes of the flames change as you watch them. If you look very hard you will see a bird with burning feathers, there, in the very heart of the brightest coals. That is the Firebird, the most beautiful bird in all the world.

But how could a bird, even a bird whose beauty shines like a flame, overcome the wicked Kostchei and defeat his evil plans? Listen carefully, my children, and I will tell you exactly what happened.

One evening then, just as the sun was setting behind the mountains to the west, Prince Ivan was wandering through the forest, trying to find his way home. All at once, he saw a wall, with apple branches nodding over it.

'Some great nobleman obviously lives here,' Prince Ivan said to himself. 'He will surely tell me where I am and how I may find my way home. I shall climb the wall and ask for help.'

Just as Prince Ivan was climbing over the wall into Kostchei's garden, he caught sight of the Firebird, flying over the orchard. Her tail feathers streamed behind her as she flew and she lit up the darkening branches with her brilliance as she passed over them. Prince Ivan immediately put an arrow to his bow and took aim, but found himself powerless to kill the beautiful creature. 'I cannot justify destroying such a magnificent bird,' he thought, 'and yet how wonderful it would be to capture her. I would look after her well, and feast my eyes on her loveliness forever.'

Prince Ivan followed the Firebird, and as she fluttered to the ground, he stalked her as silently as any cat. At last, he caught her. The poor Firebird struggled in his arms, and she cried, "Let me go, Prince Ivan. Have pity on me. I know you mean me no harm, but I will die if I am caged. How will I spread my wings?"

Prince Ivan looked at the Firebird's wings, at her gold and scarlet plumage flickering like small flames, and said, "You are quite right, beautiful bird. I shall set you free to fly and light up the night with your radiant loveliness."

The Firebird rearranged her feathers. "I shall go now, Prince Ivan, but before I do, here is my gift to you, to thank you for your kindness. It is one of my feathers, and if ever you feel that I can help you,

hold it in your hand and say these words:
Firebird, hear me.
Firebird, help me.
Firebird, appear to me.
Firebird, draw near to me.
and immediately I will be at your side."

"Thank you," said Prince Ivan, putting the feather carefully into his waistcoat pocket. Secretly, he wondered how a mere bird, however splendid, could possibly help a Royal Prince armed with the sharpest of swords, but he was a polite young man who knew his manners and so he said nothing. The Firebird rose above the tree in a bright fluttering of feathers, flew into the sky, and disappeared.

"I must find my way out of here," said the Prince to himself, but the very next instant, he saw, almost floating in the

darkness between the tree trunks, a line of young maidens dressed in white. The loveliest of the maidens came first, and led her companions in a dance around a tree that Prince Ivan had not noticed before. Every apple on this tree was made of gold and the maidens picked one of the shining fruits and tossed it in the air as though it were a ball.

Prince Ivan stepped forward out of the shadows and said to the most beautiful

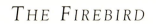

of the dancers, "My name is Prince Ivan, and I am lost in these woods. Until I saw you, I counted that as my misfortune, but now that I have seen you, I bless the fate that has brought me here to your side. Tell me your name, for I shall love you till the day I die."

The lady shook her head, "You must go at once. You must not love me, for nothing will come of it. I am the Princess Tsarevna and these are my ladies, and we are all prisoners of the sorcerer, Kostchei. This is

his enchanted garden. O, flee, Prince Ivan, flee at once, for if he catches you he will turn you to stone."

Prince Ivan said, "Only because you beg me, Tsarevna, will I flee, but I will return to rescue you and your maidens."

"Shh, do not speak," cried Tsarevna. "You must leave now. Can you not hear the trumpets? He is coming . . . oh, hurry, hurry!"

Prince Ivan turned and ran, but out of the darkness a huge, wrought-iron gate appeared and blocked his path.

"I cannot escape!" he called out to the Princess. "The gates are locked. I am doomed, for I can see him approaching." Just then, the metal gates swung open and Kostchei swept into his orchard wrapped in his long, black cloak. Behind him followed his monstrous army.

Can you picture them, my children?
Half-animal, half-human, furry, spotted,
crawling, leaping – all the creatures unlucky
enough to have fallen under Kostchei's
spell were forming a circle around
Prince Ivan.

Kostchei spoke, and his voice was like
cracking ice, and the silver daggers of his
fingernails sliced up the air.

"Who is this who dares invade the
silence of my orchard?"

"My name is Ivan," said the Prince, "and
I am not afraid of you, Kostchei."

A great murmuring and sighing rose from Kostchei's creatures, but when their master spoke, they fell silent.

"Look at this world," Kostchei said, "for soon you will be turned to stone and others will look upon you. What a fine statue your Highness will make!"

All at once, Prince Ivan remembered the feather that the Firebird had given him. He pulled it out of his waistcoat pocket and waved it high in the air, crying:

"Firebird, hear me.
Firebird, help me.
Firebird, appear to me.
Firebird, draw near to me."

Lightning zigzagged across the night sky, and there before him was the Firebird herself. Her fiery plumage dazzled the sorcerer and he shrank away from her.

She shook her feathers and spoke to Kostchei's dreadful followers, "You wish to rejoice at Prince Ivan's destruction, and to dance is to rejoice. I say you shall dance, every one of you, until you can dance no more. Now begin."

Kostchei was completely powerless, for do you not know, my children, that heat can melt even the coldest ice? So it is that Goodness will always have dominion over Evil, and when Goodness is ablaze, and on fire, then Darkness shrinks before it, and soon vanishes altogether.

The monstrous horde began to dance. They could not stop themselves. Their legs and arms whirled them around and around, faster and faster, until they could no longer stand upright. At last, they fell exhausted to the ground.

"You have danced until you have dropped," said the Firebird, "and now you shall sleep."

She rustled her beautiful golden wings in a soothing lullaby and everyone slept. Everyone, that is, except for Prince Ivan and the wicked Kostchei.

"I am immortal!" he shrieked. "You may use your magic on them, but never on me."

The Firebird laughed. "Prince Ivan, you must now act quickly. Break the egg that holds the immortal soul of this wicked enchanter. Take it from its hiding-place in the dark hollow of that tree and break it into a thousand fragments."

"Oh, no, no!" screamed Kostchei, flapping his black cloak about him. "Not my soul . . . leave me my soul. Oh, I shall die if the egg is broken!"

It was too late, Prince Ivan had found the egg, encrusted with rubies and moonstones, and thrown it to the ground with all his strength. As it cracked, the heavens were filled with thunder that could have been Kostchei roaring in the agony of his death. Utter darkness fell from the sky, and utter silence. Then a pale golden light began to creep over the horizon. Dawn was breaking, and Prince Ivan shook his head in wonder. Where were Kostchei's monsters and creatures?

What had become of Tsarevna and her maidens? The forest, the orchard, the wall, and the gate: everything had vanished, and of the Firebird not so much as a single feather remained.

Prince Ivan was in the hall of a palace, surrounded by courtiers and finely-dressed ladies. Trumpets sounded, and then, in a long line, just as they had appeared in Kostchei's garden, his beloved and her ladies came into the hall. Prince Ivan took Tsarevna's hand, and one of the courtiers said, "You have released us all from the darkness of Kostchei's enchantment. Stay and be our King and the Princess Tsarevna will be Queen."

Thus it was that Evil was banished from the land, and a new Tsar and Tsarina came to the throne of Russia. Prince Ivan never

About
the Ballets

GISELLE WAS FIRST PERFORMED at the Paris Opéra in 1841. It was choreographed by Jean Coralli for the ballerina Carlotta Grisi. The French poet, Théophile Gautier, devised the story from a German original by fellow poet, Heinrich Heine. The music is by Adolphe Adam. Giselle is a wonderful part for any female dancer, a part she dreams of throughout her long and difficult training.

Of all the arts, ballet is probably the most demanding. Not everyone has the right frame, strength or temperament to be trained as a dancer. Those who do must have a passion for ballet and the discipline that goes with it.

All dancers have to devote themselves to their training, which begins in early childhood and never ends. Even the greatest principal dancers have to attend class daily, doing many of the same exercises as the youngest beginner, in order to maintain the strength and suppleness of their bodies. Dancers must try to avoid injury, and this is why the daily class is so important: it is much easier to damage limbs that have not been thoroughly stretched and warmed-up.

The names given to the steps and exercises are in French, and wherever you learn to dance, you will use the same terms. Five foot positions must be learned, and each jump, turn and lift has its own name which is known to every dancer.

It used to be thought unmanly for boys to show an interest in ballet-dancing, but anyone who sees a video of Irek Mukhamedov or Tetsuya Kumakawa will know that a dancer requires all the power and energy we associate with the strongest athletes.

Many of the greatest dancers eventually become teachers. In this way, they pass on steps and stylistic techniques which would otherwise disappear, and the dancers of today become part of a long tradition of beauty and precision.

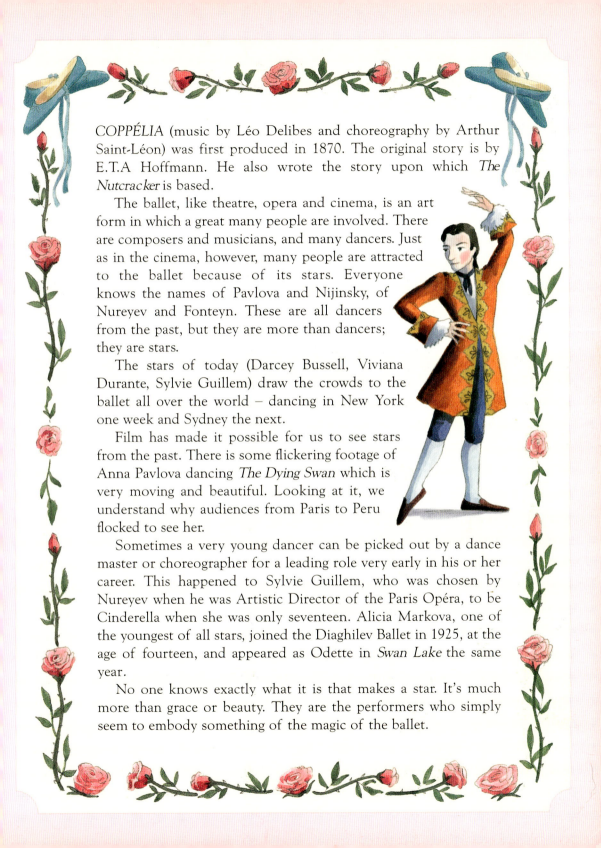

COPPÉLIA (music by Léo Delibes and choreography by Arthur Saint-Léon) was first produced in 1870. The original story is by E.T.A Hoffmann. He also wrote the story upon which *The Nutcracker* is based.

The ballet, like theatre, opera and cinema, is an art form in which a great many people are involved. There are composers and musicians, and many dancers. Just as in the cinema, however, many people are attracted to the ballet because of its stars. Everyone knows the names of Pavlova and Nijinsky, of Nureyev and Fonteyn. These are all dancers from the past, but they are more than dancers; they are stars.

The stars of today (Darcey Bussell, Viviana Durante, Sylvie Guillem) draw the crowds to the ballet all over the world – dancing in New York one week and Sydney the next.

Film has made it possible for us to see stars from the past. There is some flickering footage of Anna Pavlova dancing *The Dying Swan* which is very moving and beautiful. Looking at it, we understand why audiences from Paris to Peru flocked to see her.

Sometimes a very young dancer can be picked out by a dance master or choreographer for a leading role very early in his or her career. This happened to Sylvie Guillem, who was chosen by Nureyev when he was Artistic Director of the Paris Opéra, to be Cinderella when she was only seventeen. Alicia Markova, one of the youngest of all stars, joined the Diaghilev Ballet in 1925, at the age of fourteen, and appeared as Odette in *Swan Lake* the same year.

No one knows exactly what it is that makes a star. It's much more than grace or beauty. They are the performers who simply seem to embody something of the magic of the ballet.

SWAN LAKE WAS FIRST produced in 1877. The music was by Tchaikovsky, and the production was a failure. In 1894, after the composer's death, the ballet was revived with new choreography by Marius Petipa, and was a great success. Today, it is probably the best-known of all ballets.

Although you will often hear of daring experiments with plays – of Hamlet set in a prison, or Romeo and Juliet on the streets of New York – it is rarer for a ballet to be staged in a non-traditional way, although this is sometimes done.

There are, of course, many modern ballets which take place not in a sort of fairyland but in the real, recognizable world. *The Judas Tree*, for instance, takes place on a building site.

It is possible for classical ballets to be staged in different kinds of spaces: in the round, in school halls, in tents and so forth. But ballet companies have their homes, for the most part, in beautiful theatres which date back to the last century or earlier.

The Paris Opéra, right in the heart of the city, is a magnificent building. Inside, there are wide staircases, marble columns and all 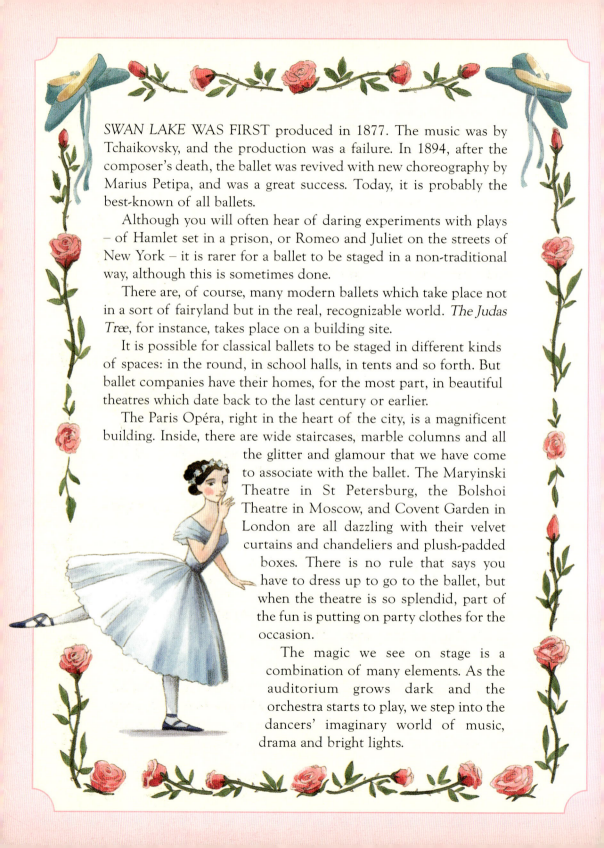 the glitter and glamour that we have come to associate with the ballet. The Maryinski Theatre in St Petersburg, the Bolshoi Theatre in Moscow, and Covent Garden in London are all dazzling with their velvet curtains and chandeliers and plush-padded boxes. There is no rule that says you have to dress up to go to the ballet, but when the theatre is so splendid, part of the fun is putting on party clothes for the occasion.

The magic we see on stage is a combination of many elements. As the auditorium grows dark and the orchestra starts to play, we step into the dancers' imaginary world of music, drama and bright lights.

THE SLEEPING BEAUTY WAS first put on in 1890. The music was by Tchaikovsky and the choreography by Marius Petipa. The fairytale is a very ancient one, but it was first written down in the eighteenth century by a Frenchman called Charles Perrault.

The choreographer of a ballet decides which steps should be danced on stage and in which order. They are responsible for the overall pattern of the ballet, and every individual step taken by each member of the cast.

There have been many famous choreographers. The work of Petipa, Nijinsky and Fokine can still be seen today, as their ideas have passed down to a new generation of choreographers who have danced the steps themselves. Modern choreographers like to add something of their own and make changes to well-known works, but one can still see ballets danced today that are very like those of a century ago.

Swan Lake, The Sleeping Beauty and *La Bayadère* are all the creations of Marius Petipa, the most famous choreographer of the Imperial Russian period. He worked very closely with Tchaikovsky on *The Nutcracker,* but was prevented from choreographing this ballet because of illness.

You could say that the choreography is an extension of the music, the spirit of the music made visible. If the choreographer sees qualities in a dancer which they would like to develop and emphasise, they can create a whole ballet around that particular person's skills.

Choreographers have to keep in their heads not only each single dancer's movements, but the way in which a whole company of people uses the stage and fills it with constantly changing patterns. By the time we see the ballet, they are a part of the magic and seem to have grown naturally from the music.

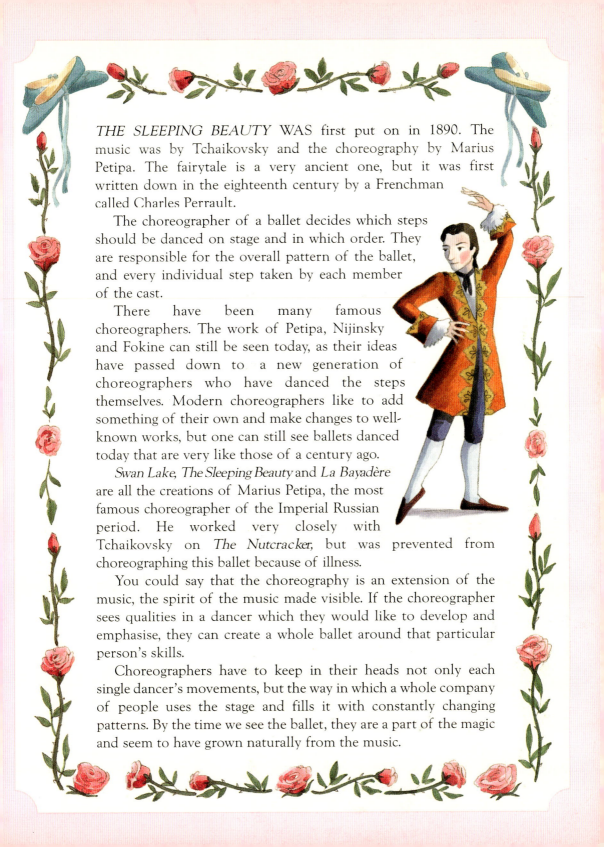

THE NUTCRACKER WAS PERFORMED for the first time in 1892. It was choreographed first by Petipa and then by Lev Ivanov after Petipa fell ill. The story is by Hoffmann, and the music was the last great ballet score written by Tchaikovsky before his death.

You can dance to any music as long as it has a strong, definite rhythm. There have been ballets set to jazz, rock'n'roll, and many classical pieces that were not written especially for the dance. For example, the ballet, *Les Sylphides* can also be called *Chopiniana* because Fokine choreographed it as a physical embodiment of music of Chopin.

Sometimes the composer tries to express a story, or a scene that the choreographer has visualized. Tchaikovsky was supremely skilled at doing this, and so was Stravinsky, who wrote the score for *The Firebird*. Prokofiev is another famous composer whose *Romeo and Juliet* is still performed by every major ballet company. There is a beautiful version of it on video, danced by Rudolf Nureyev and Margot Fonteyn.

Music written for ballet has to do some of the same things as film music. It has to help to convey a certain atmosphere. It tells us the mood we are supposed to be in. Some ballet music is so well-known that we associate it with other things. Advertisers often use ballet music in their jingles and ballet music is frequently played in school for such things as walking into and out of assembly. It comes as a delightful surprise when you see your first ballet and recognize a melody you know transformed by being a part of a beautiful whole.

Music does far more than provide a background for the dancing. It is the transformation of what the composer has written into what we hear that casts the first spell. The music is where the magic begins.

THE FIREBIRD WAS FIRST produced in 1910 as part of Diaghilev's second season in Paris. The story is an old Russian legend. The choreography is by Fokine, and the music was Stravinsky's first ballet score. The set and costumes were by Golovin, and the costumes of the Firebird and the Princess were designed by Bakst.

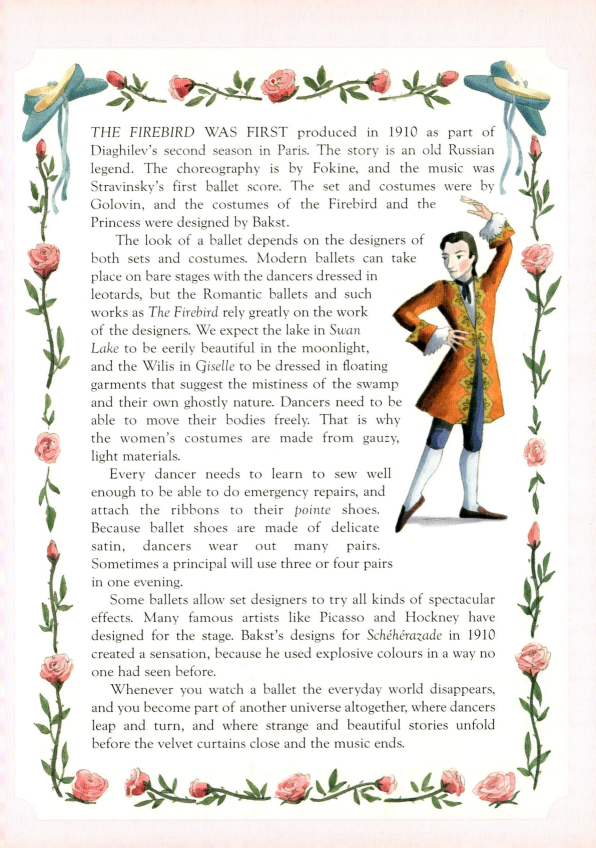

The look of a ballet depends on the designers of both sets and costumes. Modern ballets can take place on bare stages with the dancers dressed in leotards, but the Romantic ballets and such works as *The Firebird* rely greatly on the work of the designers. We expect the lake in *Swan Lake* to be eerily beautiful in the moonlight, and the Wilis in *Giselle* to be dressed in floating garments that suggest the mistiness of the swamp and their own ghostly nature. Dancers need to be able to move their bodies freely. That is why the women's costumes are made from gauzy, light materials.

Every dancer needs to learn to sew well enough to be able to do emergency repairs, and attach the ribbons to their *pointe* shoes. Because ballet shoes are made of delicate satin, dancers wear out many pairs. Sometimes a principal will use three or four pairs in one evening.

Some ballets allow set designers to try all kinds of spectacular effects. Many famous artists like Picasso and Hockney have designed for the stage. Bakst's designs for *Schéhérazade* in 1910 created a sensation, because he used explosive colours in a way no one had seen before.

Whenever you watch a ballet the everyday world disappears, and you become part of another universe altogether, where dancers leap and turn, and where strange and beautiful stories unfold before the velvet curtains close and the music ends.